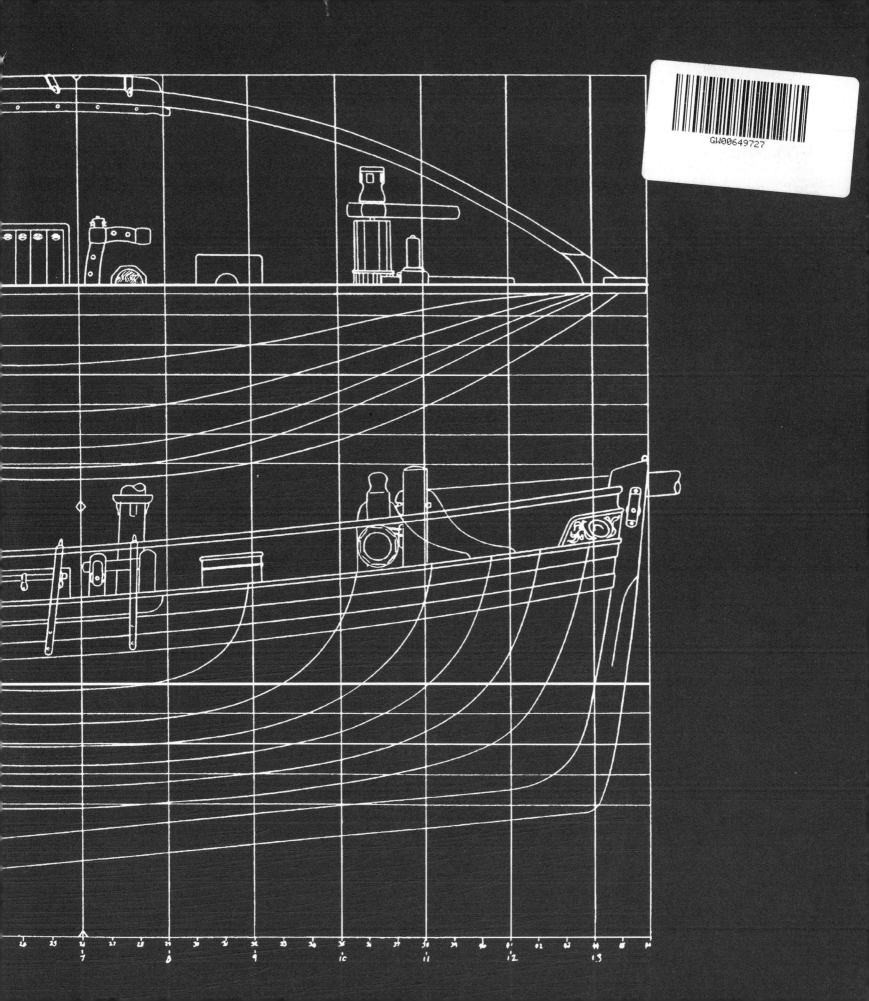

To Joanna my love.

And to my parents Tony & Simonetta
for showing me a better life,

and Alan Reekie
for giving me the right attitude
to work.

First published in an edition
of 1,000 copies in 2012 by

The Dovecote Press Ltd
Stanbridge, Wimborne Minster
Dorset BH21 4JD
www.dovecotepress.com

ISBN 978-0-9573119-1-6

1 3 5 7 9 8 6 4 2

Designed & typeset by

Christian Topf Design Ltd
Falmouth, Cornwall, TR11 3LL
www.ctd-studio.co.uk

Printed in Singapore by

KHL Printing Pte Ltd
Singapore 508968
www.khlprint.com

All papers used by The Dovecote
Press are natural, recyclable products
made from wood grown in sustainable,
well-managed forests.

Working Sail Ltd
Gweek, Cornwall, TR12 6UF
www.workingsail.co.uk

AUTHOR'S NOTE

*All the photographs in the early chapters, including Greece, Faversham and Charmian, were taken
on cheap primitive cameras, many of them on the Box 'Brownie' given to me by mother when I
was ten. Since then they have lived a rough life, always travelling with me, either from boat to
boat, or in an old leather bag when hitchhiking to and fro across Europe. They have survived all
my near sinkings, as well as seawater, wind, sun and rain. It is a miracle that I have managed
to hang on to them. We decided not to try and artificially 'improve' them on a computer,
but let them speak for themselves. So please forgive their quality. Every scratch tells a story!*

LUKE POWELL

Working Sail

A LIFE IN WOODEN BOATS

The Dovecote Press

6 **Forewords**

10 **Introduction**

Chapter 1
20 **Greece**

Chapter 2
36 **Faversham**

Chapter 3
48 **Charmian**

Chapter 4
62 **To Build a Boat – Eve**

Chapter 5
76 **Lizzie May**

Chapter 6
92 **Agnes**

Contents

Chapter 7
110 **Hesper**

Chapter 8
126 **Rebirth of Lizzie**

Chapter 9
140 **Ezra**

Chapter 10
156 **Return of Agnes**

Chapter 11
170 **Tallulah**

Chapter 12
186 **Amelie Rose**

Appendix One
204 **The Regattas & Beyond**

Appendix Two
216 **Pilot Cutters of the Scillies**

236 Glossary

238 Acknowledgements

239 List of Subscribers

FOREWORD by TOM CUNLIFFE

Luke has researched his subject as thoroughly as anyone alive and his boats stand out in any seascape as the loveliest of all.

I first met Luke Powell twenty years or so ago at a classic boat regatta. He and a few mates were careering round the moored craft in a heavily canvassed cutter of unusual beauty called *Charmian*. They were having a whale of a time and a lot of folks in the anchorage were casting beady eyes on them hoping they wouldn't get out of control near *their* yachts. They needn't have worried. These guys knew their business. I didn't realise then that Luke would turn out to be a master boatbuilder and a great artist to boot.

The next time we met was in Exeter while he was building *Lizzie May* and I was commissioned to write an article on the boat. When I saw her, she was a shell without much accommodation and two things struck me. The first was what a joy it is just to lie down among the timbers of an empty wooden boat and feel the harmony all around. The second was a sense of admiration for a man who, in a world driven largely by what sells at boat shows, was prepared to put his soul on the line for what he believed in. Many non-race boats of today are designed and built with accommodation as first priority. Huge aft cabins with island beds impress at Earl's Court or Excel; they work in marinas too, but try using one in the North Atlantic hard on the wind in force six. No, thank you very much, has to be the seaman's response. Luke Powell's boats are obviously created primarily to be at one with the environment in which they are built to serve. The accommodation goes in afterwards. It is this understanding of what really matters that makes such vessels the most comfortable and safe of all.

His eye is extraordinary, but it never compromises the critical factor of how the boat swims on the water.

The men who built Scillonian pilot cutters in the nineteenth century knew not only how to make a boat that would do their job, they also must have cared about how she looked. Luke has researched his subject as thoroughly as anyone alive and his boats stand out in any seascape as the loveliest of all. His eye is extraordinary, but it never compromises the critical factor of how the boat swims on the water. I loved the account in this book about bringing *Agnes* from America. Her passage time was similar to the one I made in my own gaff cutter *Westernman* when we sailed her from Cape Cod to Falmouth. Like her, we had three reefs in for much of the time, yet still we flew onwards. The photograph of Bishop Rock on a rough, grey day says it all. The Bishop

remains the most romantic landfall in the world for me. For Luke and his crew, sailing their pilot cutter home across the mighty wilderness to where she must long to be, I know it will never be forgotten.

Luke Powell has done us all a favour by writing this book. Tell your friends about it, leave a copy in the marina office so that those who do not yet understand can be brought to a richer life through its pages. Who knows, maybe some of them, too, will leave the consumer world behind and find a boat that is at peace on the great waters.

Tom Cunliffe
2012

FOREWORD by JEREMY IRONS

The seas were big and the wind delightfully strong as I felt Agnes muscle into the waves ...

At the furthermost tip of south-western Ireland, between peninsulas that reach out to the Atlantic like fingers, lies Roaring Water Bay. Surprisingly, not named for its own nature, but rather after the tumbling river which spews its roaring waters into the sea at the bay's landward end. Guarded by Clear Island, the bay is peppered with other, smaller outcrops, some peopled, others deserted but for crumbling ruins, hardy flocks of sheep and the occasional goat; visited in fair weather for their little beaches, but avoided in foul, as are the unpredictable rocks which lurk just below or above the tide. Ten miles out to the horizon lies the Fastnet Rock with its famed lighthouse, and beyond that, America and much of the Irish diaspora.

From time to time I live in a tower house on one of those small islands on the edge of the bay, and on a clear night I can lie, one hundred feet above the sea, enjoying the beam sweeping from the Fastnet playing on the walls around my bed with its unchanging rhythm.

The morning has never been my best of times, but when I'm there my first joy is to peer out of the uncurtained windows to see how the new day has dawned. Sun, cloud, or rain, and what weather the sky and wind direction predict for the remains of the day.

One such summer morning I was greeted by the sight of a pair of what I judged to be Brixham trawlers, the *Hesper* and the *Agnes*, a long way from home, and moored in the lee of my island. Few boats venture this far inland, for to do so means negotiating the ubiquitous mussel lines crisscrossing much of the bay, but advertising, by their presence, the pureness of its waters.

So these silent visitors, for at this hour there was no one stirring above decks, were a welcome sight. Traditional sailing boats built of wood and rigged in sisal and canvas have become a rarity, as we succumb to the easy maintenance of plastics and glass-fibre, and, in my experience, the men and women who sail them can be some of life's most interesting.

A few miles away, on the banks of the Ilen River my friends Liam and John Hegarty who twenty years ago built my gaff-rigged ketch in the yard where their father worked before them, are rebuilding ,and sometimes building anew, traditional Irish workboats, and as you explore this coastline you come across examples of their work nestling up in sheltered bays.

But that morning's visitors were bigger than our local workboats; well able to withstand the ocean in its foulest moods. They dwarfed my little ketch moored nearby, and as I looked longingly at their lines, honed by generations of maritime experience, their crew began to stir.

In my experience, however well provisioned and kitted out a boat is, after a sea voyage its crew always welcomes the chance to enjoy the comforts afforded on land.

... glorying in her own splendour, with **Hesper** rising and falling beside us as we vied for speed and trim.

And so it was no surprise that my invitation to showers and a full Irish breakfast were accepted with alacrity as I gave directions where to come ashore. And while we crowded into my little kitchen and downed coffee, eggs, bacon, black and white pudding, toast and marmalade, I was introduced to this extraordinary man, Luke Powell, who had built, and his family and friends that were crewing, the two boats swinging at anchor fifty foot below my kitchen window.

Later that morning, hunger assuaged and bodies freshened, we set sail down the bay, and out towards the Fastnet Rock. The seas were big and the wind delightfully strong as I felt *Agnes* muscle into the waves, glorying in her own splendour, with *Hesper* rising and falling beside us as we vied for speed and trim. And as we rounded the Fastnet, with the white spume thundering against the rocks only metres away from us, I felt both privileged and protected aboard this magnificent sailing vessel.

For those who have never experienced such sensations, I would exhort them to seek them out. This wonderful volume may whet your appetite. And for all of us, even the saltiest of sea-dogs, perusing these pages on a winter's night will allow us to marvel at the wonders of the past, and, perhaps, dream of wondrous voyages to come.

Jeremy Irons
2012

Three coasting barges at the Chain Locker Quay, Falmouth, in 1939. These were cutter-rigged barges that traded to the many quays in the rivers of south Cornwall, from the Tamar to Truro River and up the Helford to Gweek Quay.

INTRODUCTION

At this time the creeks, inlets & marshes were full of old derelicts. You could find wooden boats dying everywhere: sailing barges, wherries, trading ketches, fishing smacks, steam trawlers, gentlemans' yachts, old wartime MTB's.

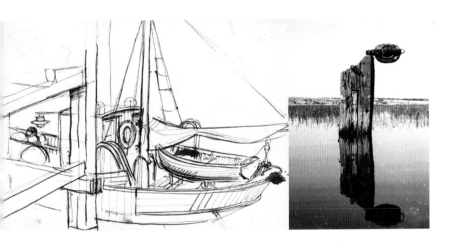

Facing page: *Mast of an Ile de Groix tunnyman, near Lorient in France. The complete fleet was scuttled by the Nazis to stop people sailing across the Channel to join the Free French. These beautiful vessels still lie there in the mud, waiting to be dug out and sailed again.*

Above left: *Sketch by my father of the fishing boat he worked on in Newhaven during 1948.*

Above right: *The stem of a sailing barge complete with wooden stay-fall block. All that remains of the Pride now stands alone with her hull fallen away, in the marshes of the Swale near Harty Ferry, Kent.*

All of my life I have been totally wrapped up in the world of wooden boats, enthusiastically raking through the dying embers of a great age that has passed into history. There is little residue of all that once was, only a few old photos, some scraps of paper and the odd gravestone – all their fine ships are no more. But reading the autobiography of a bygone schooner captain opens a window onto a lost world, giving an insight into the ways of the past and illuminating the people that stood here before us. Unfortunately, few wrote of their lives, leaving nothing of themselves to pass on. When researching the pilot cutters from the Isles of Scilly I would have given my left leg to have read something written by the men who built them, thus opening a door for me to peer through. Yet there is nothing.

Maybe some time in the future a young lad attempting to restore an old boat will want to reflect on the lives of those who preceded him but shared his enthusiasm. Hopefully, I may, in a little way, help fuel his passion for the wooden boat. If so, this book will have served its purpose.

What is it about the wooden sailing ship that stirs one's soul? There are times in our collective history – noble events, great deeds of exploration, and feats of engineering – that inspire us. The one thing that combines all these elements and turns lofty dreams into a wondrous reality is the wooden sailing ship. Through the craftsmanship and industrious labour required to build it, to the skill and courage it takes to sail it out into the open seas. Man and machine is pitted against all that nature has to offer.

It was thanks to my father that I learned to appreciate wooden working boats and become passionate for all that they stood for. He had returned from the Second World War as a young

Left: *Spritsail barges at Pin Mill on the River Orwell, Suffolk, in the late 1970s. There were then dozens of barges on the foreshore, some rigged and running, others as houseboats and the rest derelict or being restored.*

Below left: *Deck view of a Cornish coasting barge.*

Below right: *Coasting barges awaiting cargo in Hooe Lake, Plymouth, in the 1930s.*

man deeply disturbed by what he had witnessed. One of the first people to walk into Belsen after its liberation, the experience had a profound affect on him. As a way of healing, he threw himself into hard physical work, apprenticing as a fisherman and going to sea in a vessel called the *Little Mint* working out of Newhaven on the south coast.

In the post-war years fishing was tough. The rewards were meagre. The fishermen my father sailed with were an insular and embittered people and did their best to make his life as difficult as possible in an attempt to drive him away. But he was not easily shifted, and in due course was able to buy his own boat. In time the family grew and he decided to step ashore. But his respect for the sea and boats never left him. He handed all this down to me through many wonderful stories. I was enthralled and soaked them up like a sponge. What is it that brings a man to a place? Why is it that some people end up bankers, farmers, mountaineers, or fishermen? On my father's knee the tide was set and I was hooked.

My childhood was spent in Suffolk. On rainy winter days he took me down to the blustery pier head at Lowestoft to watch stout wooden trawlers bravely putting to sea, bludgeoning out through steep waves, to disappear in a flurry of spray. This taught me the nobility of the working boat facing all that the elements could throw at her, simply going to sea to earn her daily crust.

They say that the experiences of our childhood help shape our future. Rather than play football with the other kids I would explore the waterfront, the derelict quays, and the Suffolk marshes. It was my secret world. I walked miles in search of old vessels that could tell of their lives on the high seas, and the more I searched the more I gained a taste for these old ships that oozed history.

*We were weighing anchor on the sailing barge
Scotsman when the Whitstable smack* Rose
& Ada *came out of the early morning mist
at the start of the Swale Match 1981.*

At this time the creeks, inlets, and marshes of England were full of old derelicts. You could find wooden boats dying everywhere: sailing barges, wherries, trading ketches, topsail schooners, fishing smacks, steam trawlers, gentlemans' yachts, old wartime MTB's, and MFV's.

Once a vessel had served a useful life it would be laid to rest in the soft mud to gently fall apart. After the war there had been a shortage of housing and these vessels made good homes. Many old boats were tied up in the marshes to have sheds built upon them, with reclaimed sash windows, pot plants, smoking chimneys, washing hanging and long rickety walkways to the towpath.

This was the late 1960s and plastic boats had not as yet invaded my world. It was still a time when it was exciting to walk around harbours, taking delight in the vessels one saw. Even at nine years of age I would walk for miles in search of an interesting vessel. If unoccupied I would climb aboard, looking at every detail, trying to work out how she would have been when rigged and sailing. If there was an open porthole or hatchway I would climb inside to discover her workings.

Turning a bend in a creek my heart would leap at the sight of an old trading ketch or schooner, or the bones of long abandoned ships buried in the marshes. I suppose it was a form of archaeology. It felt all the more valuable to me because it seemed so unappreciated and about to be lost. Rounding a corner I once found a line of ten houseboats converted from a Victorian steam yacht, a Boomie barge, a sailing trawler and some big Victorian racing cutters, all cut down and built upon with sheds and the usual clutter of live-aboard life. Excitedly, I ran from one to the next, looking up in wonder at the beautiful carved scroll work on the clipper bows, squelching through the mud under the long ornate counters trying to read their names through the years of accumulated flaking paint.

Finally exhausted I sat down on the bank of the towpath, still taking stock, when I heard a couple walking by tut tutting, 'what an eye sore, when will they clear these horrid things away, a vile mess.' Bang! This brought me down to earth with a bump. How can people think so differently? How can they not see the beauty in these relics from another age? Sadly, as I have grown older, such people have had their way and have tidied up our world. The Norfolk wherries, the Lowestoft steam drifters, the Thames sailing barges, the sailing trawlers, and the West Country schooners have all been broken up and burnt – leaving the world a blander place.

Old steamers, a sailing cutter & coasting barge as houseboats. West Mersea, Shoreham and on the beach at Falmouth where there is now a Marina.

Above: *My father beneath the stern of the Rosa & Ada at Whitstable when she was just out of trade. Father was inspecting her with a viewing to purchasing her so that we could sail away to Greece. This is 1967, and one of my early attempts at photography with a Box 'Brownie'.*

St Andreas worked out of the island of Aegina, carrying building materials from Piraeus to ports and islands around the Peloponnese. Note the sawn off bowsprit as well as the missing mainmast, cut off to make room for a mechanical sand grab. Yet still she carries sails on the foremast.

ΑΓ. ΑΝΔΡΕΑΣ ΠΑΤ 262

GREECE

As time went on, wanderlust took hold of my parents. They had met at the Slade School of Art before the war, and both retained a bohemian hunger for freedom. Tired of domestic routine and the unending vista of provincial life they decided to set sail for the Aegean, to make life count.

Above: *Mum and dad in a café at Paralia on the Peloponnese. Time for an ouzo.* **Right:** *Traders of all sizes at Mykonos. The inner vessel in the foreground still carries both masts and a full rig.*

Spetsai old harbour 70

In the winter of 1967 father purchased an old Scottish fishing boat, *Thistle*, built in the 1920's on the lines of a type of sailing boat called the Zulu. At 40 feet in length she was small and tatty but with a bit of work she was made into a good home and in the spring of 1969 the family was packed aboard, pets and all, and we set sail for Greece. My sister was seven, I nine, and my older brother fourteen, but despite the uncertainty all three of us were swept along by our parent's enthusiasm.

The idea was to stay away from England until the money ran out. We cruised around the Greek islands retracing the voyage of Ulysses, on an Odyssey to discover places untouched by the modern world. We anchored in wild bays, snorkelled and dived in crystal clear waters, returning to the surface grinning

Above & below: *My mother's drawings of the old harbour at Spetses and a caique loaded with bricks at Poros.*

Right: *Traders alongside in the old harbour of Spetses. Captains' houses look down on the quay.*

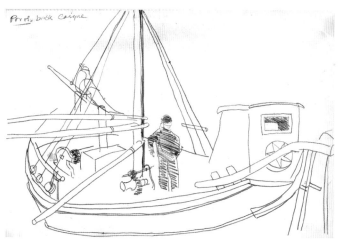

Poros brick caique

excitedly and clutching amphora from ancient wrecks. On other days we climbed in the hills to explore classical Greek ruins, as yet hidden from tourists, often battling through thorn and scrub to search them out. Scrambling high up, we skipped across the sun-bleached rocks like mountain goats, chasing lizards and catching baby tortoises. Taking delight in all the wonders we found, we adapted to our new life with the natural enthusiasm of children.

As winter came it was decided to settle on the small island of Spetses, which lay close to the mainland and had a safe harbour. The island had been home to a great fleet of merchantmen, mainly brigs of 200 to 300 tons, which once plied the waters of the eastern Mediterranean. There were also smaller vessels, lateen rigged of between 50 to 80 feet. Of these, nearly all had gone, yet still there remained traces of their world. Big elegant captains' houses full of paintings of sailing ships looked down on a quayside paved with stones polished by age and furnished with cannons buried upright as mooring posts.

On the far side of the harbour stood old warehouses with vaulted ceilings, and at the seaward end were high stone-walled sail-lofts, silent and crumbling. Between the buildings lay a beach still used as a slipway for the hauling out of everything from a little rowing boat being repainted by an elderly moustachioed fisherman, to the great lumbering mass of a wooden cargo carrier.

The slipway functioned by using two great baulks of timber that were slid under the full length of the vessel, like a great sledge with the keel sitting between them. Stout iron bars were driven thwart-ships at each end to connect the baulks. The sledge was weighted with lumps of scrap iron and pushed out into the sea to sink. The vessel would be manouvered into position by men heaving at ropes, all shouting and pulling in different directions. Once grounded on the sledge a long-suffering mule was goaded into action. Round and round went the capstan. Slowly imperceptibly the great mass would start to rise out of the water, the wire running back and forth through pulley blocks, giving this one mule the power to lift a great ship. As she rose out of the water, wedges were driven under the bilges to help spread the load and sleepers, basted in hot tallow, were placed in its path to guide her up the beach.

One of the slipyards in the old harbour of Spetses servicing all manner of craft. The baulks of timber, weighted with chain, were used to slip the boats.

Above: *The* Eleni *supplied the island of Hydra once a week with household wares – everything from tinned foods to bottled drinks, bedsteads to toilet paper, ouzo to nails – the entire island's needs. It was all unloaded by hand and carried away by donkey.*
Below: *Loading paving stone at Karystos for Mykonos. The anchor hangs from it's cathead in the manner of old.*

Above: *An old timer on it's way from Piraeus to Monemvasia. Note how slowly the engine drives her.*
Below: *Another view of Eleni unloading at Hydra. Yorgos comes away carrying his packages.*

The men running the yard gradually got used to me, though they remained much amused at this young boy from a far off land trying to help and yet getting in their way. I had my uses though. On launch day they would despatch me in the ancient shipyard punt to chase after the wedges as they floated free. I was never happier than when sitting with my legs dangling over the edge of the quay watching life go by.

Then one day I heard the slow donk, donk, donk of a big single cylinder Bolinder semi diesel. My heart leapt in anticipation. Rounding the headland, deeply laden and decks awash, came a wooden three masted topsail schooner of about 90 feet, with beautiful lines and the wonderful sheer of a great sailor. Though the bowsprit was hacked short, the masts sawn off at deck level, with just the lower foremast remaining to set a gaff and few jibs to steady her, I could not believe my eyes. It was as if I had fallen through a wormhole in space and landed in another time, a paradise where sailing ships still lived.

The captain stood aft high on a thwart, steering the tiller with rope and tackle. As she glided in towards the stone quay a crewman disappeared down the companionway scuttle. The engine slowed almost to a stop, the heavy flywheel bounced on the last compression, then with the fuel opened up the engine gathered speed backwards, donk donk donk, puffing large blue smoke rings high into the sky. Gradually, the vessel lost way. One could feel the great inertia, a belly full of cargo, as the single cylinder puffed and the prop deep below her stern pulled at the water. Heaving lines with 'Turks heads' were thrown ashore and slowly she was warped alongside. The crew worked quietly, each knowing his task. Then began the work of getting her ready to land the cargo. Hatch covers were taken off, the derrick shipped and once a blowlamp had been lit to heat the head of the donkey engine, its flywheel was swung, bursting into life.

Horse carts arrived and finally the cargo, slung in a canvas strop, was lifted from the hold, and swung high in the sky before being lowered onto the carts. The cargo changed as they

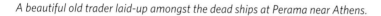

A beautiful old trader laid-up amongst the dead ships at Perama near Athens.

Two vessels that worked out of Aegina. The closest is Panagia, *who carried building sand and bricks from Piraeus to the islands, whilst behind her is the* Kontnos Eleni, *half loaded with empty gas bottles.*

worked through the hold, from bricks to bedsteads, lampshades to nails, anything the island needed. Hour after hour the men toiled in the hot sun as the horses peacefully chewed at their nose-bags and the carts creaked on their springs.

Then it was siesta time and all went quiet, except for me and a mad dog. I climbed aboard the ship to examine her every detail – the carved fielding on the poop deck rise, the panelled cabin top, the fluting around the mast boom table, the ornate wooden catheads over the bow, the massive patent barrel windlass, the barley twist tiller, and the carved wooden rope work around the stern. The scale of her was beyond all measure. Everything bore the influence of great ships of the past. The men that built her knew the brigs and clippers of our forefathers, working in the language of the wooden sailing ship and building from a tradition that came out of the mists of time.

Suddenly siesta was over and the men returned to work, their normally sunburnt faces white with brick dust. The vessel rose higher in the water. In time her hold was emptied, then swept, and finally the decks washed down before all became quiet again. The next morning her berth was empty. The bird had flown as if she had never existed, but her space did not stay empty for long. Another fine vessel would arrive and once again my head would spin at this new apparition. I could never believe my eyes that such things still existed.

One morning a big 'Perama' came in. The donkey winch was set up, puffing its blue smoke rings as it took the strain. Up from the hold, through the small dark hole of the hatch, came a canvas strop bearing a massive heifer, its legs kicking, snorting in anger and indignation. The derrick was swung out across the quay and the cow lowered to the ground, the vessel swaying as the weight came off the derrick.

This went on until there was a complete herd on the quay. Then lads in bare feet with sticks drove them off down the street, leaving behind a carpet of dung which was swept into the harbour, leaving the smooth flags wet and polished like marble.

After a good storm had blown through, the water in Spetses harbour was beautifully clear. I'd row to and fro in the shipyard punt, peering through a glass bottomed bucket to see what treasures lay on the seabed. Using a fisherman's grapple I

watch chain, waxed moustache, trilby and shiny shoes. He walked to the end of the quay, where half a dozen big traders were laid up stern first; bow anchors out to the far shore and their high clipper bows pushing halfway across the harbour. Kapitano Staviros climbed into a punt, pulled across to the boarding ladder of one of the schooners, and clambered up. A small man, he vanished behind the high bulwarks and topgallant rails, so that all I could see was his trilby moving about the deck. A motor pump burst into life. Water poured across the deck and out through the scuppers.

Fruit caiques at Aegina. Once a week they came across from the Peloponnese. As soon as they had tied up, the islanders climbed aboard to do their shopping.

soon built up quite a collection of deadeyes, shackles, bits of rigging – even two cannon balls. This outdoor world was my classroom, not the mornings aboard our boat with my mother patiently trying to teach us mathematics or geometry. Outside, my young eyes observed everything.

I remember a small dapper man in his late seventies who intrigued me. Kapitano Staviros lived in one of the fine houses overlooking the harbour. Every Sunday after church he would come down in his Sunday best, buttoned up waistcoat with

Staviros walked about inspecting his vessel as if getting ready for sea, before sitting down on the cargo-hatch and leaning on his walking stick, lost in memories of when his ship and he were young, of the crews that sailed with him, and of the captains of the other ships now laid up alongside. After a time the pump would run dry and cut his train of thought. He walked over and stopped the engine then threw a piece of sailcloth over it, before clambering back into the punt and rowing ashore. As time went by this dapper little gentleman

and his big old schooner grew more tired. The Teredo worms ate at her planking and she took on more water. Each week she would settle, and then with the pump, rise up again. These pumping sessions became more sporadic and she gradually settled more deeply before being emptied. One day his son Yanni came to do the job. The Kapitano had passed away in the night. Sometime later this fine ship was towed out to sea and scuttled. Master and ship died together.

At the top end of the harbour was Sam Barkly's house. He was an Englishman who had skippered an MTB during the war, hiding from the Germans in remote bays before slipping out to sink passing ships. After the war he returned with a Cornish three masted topsail schooner and began trading between the islands. Now, twenty years on, he had a fine Greek schooner called *Stormy Seas*. Originally built to replace the three master, soon after launching she was requisitioned

Above: *Bows and sterns at Mykonos and the* Agios Georgios *awaits her next cargo at the islands of Aegina.*

Below: *The Perama* Panagia *newly arrived at Poros, fully loaded with bags of lime. The sails are still loose.*

Right: *The Perama* AgGeorgios B *bringing building sand and bricks to the island of Hydra. The shape of the anchors is very eighteenth century.*

by the British Navy to run spies behind the Iron Curtain into remote parts of Albania. One legacy from these cloak-and-dagger missions were some bullets embedded in the mainmast, a prize that left me with a swipe around the head, when, with a large knife I was caught trying to extract one. Some years later, I ended up part of the schooner's crew when she was owned by Peter Throckmorton, the marine archaeologist. I still remember one charter with nubile, topless French girls climbing the ratlines to jump into the sea – a most disconcerting pleasure for a still growing boy!

As I was now a familiar sight around Spetses harbour I became more involved with the locals, helping fishermen pull their nets ashore and taking the lines for incoming traders. I even went on one of the scuttling trips as yet another wooden schooner was sent to the deep. I felt a need to witness as much as possible, I knew this was the end of an era.

Above: *The* Kostantis *unloading lime at Paralia on the Peloponnese. A wheelhouse had been built on top of the coachroof after her mainmast was removed.*

Right: Agios Ioannis *was one of the traders that would arrive at Spetses blowing smoke rings and bringing general supplies. Note the ornate carving on her stern.*

My mother, a fine artist, loved drawing the things she saw. Like me she had a thirst to observe it all, from the biblical scenes of donkeys working in the hills, threshing the corn in the ancient way, to the horse-taxis in the streets, to the arrival of the fruit boats with old ladies tottering up the gang plank to barter for their produce, and the romantic sight of the nomadic sponge divers in their beautifully painted boats, all was a feast for the eyes. Then one day my mother gave me a Box Brownie, a camera! I too could record the things I saw. She taught me how to develop negatives, turning my interest into a quest for photos. Now if I saw the sail of a trader heading for the island,

letting its blood splash over the keel to ward off evil spirits.

Quickly the frames were set up, then the planking and deck beams. Everything turned bright orange from the red lead paint that was mixed at the chandler's shop from great barrels of turpentine, linseed oil and kegs of red lead powder – the smell of this place still lingers with me today.

On launch day all the families came out in their finest. The priest, with his tall black hat, long beard, and incense swinging on a chain gave a blessing. With bouzoukis playing, and after downing a small glass of sickly sweet liqueur and

Antonios *half loaded with paving stones at Karystos. Note the aft chain plates where once a proud mainmast stood. A fine sight she must have been!*

I would run to the headland in hope of taking a photograph of her rounding into harbour with her sails still set.

The island of Spetses, though in decline as a trading port, still had a vibrant boatbuilding industry. Four yards in the old harbour were busy turning out fishing boats. Perched on the rocky foreshore, wherever there was a flat spot big enough to lay a keel, a boat was built. Some of these were high up on terraces, others on a small patch of beach between rocky outcrops. With the stem up, and a cross nailed to it, the local priest would sacrifice a chicken,

sweet cakes, we took up positions round the boat to be launched and pushed – and down the ways she went. The new kapitano would be at the tiller, his moustache twitching with pride. Putt, putt, putt, the engine started and off she went to the quay to gather her nets aboard. The next day another keel was laid.

These fishing boats were of all sizes, from pretty little open rowing boats to big Seine netters. At nights I would climb amongst their timbers. The topsides and deck were built before the bottom planking went in and this allowed me

Below: *Mother's drawing of boatbuilding in Spetses. The boats are laid over to facilitate the planking of the bottom.*

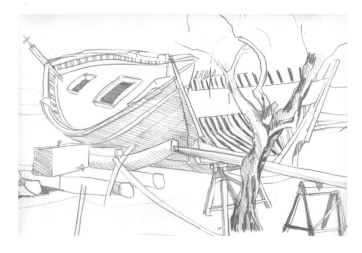

Top right: *Looking out over the harbour of Spetses.*
Below: *Yani the shipwright eyes his work, the old harbour, Spetses.*

to crawl under the bilges on a carpet of adze chippings and squeeze between her floor timbers, up into the smell of new wood. I followed the build progress keenly, aware of every stage, watching the shipwrights at work. They did everything with a hand adze. It seemed the whole boat was built with this one tool. These vessels were put together with ease – no fuss, men with a quiet knowledge handed down through the family, from father to son. I needed to soak up some of this knowledge, hoping it would stand me in good stead for the future.

Then finally the time came for us to return home, we had to sail away, leaving this beautiful island to go back to England and reality. My parents, all of us, were bewitched by what we had seen, we had tasted the ambrosia of the Gods and our thirst was not sated, we needed to drink some more. My parents, like Odysseus, were determined to return. Once in England a house was bought and sold, and a new boat built and fitted out. Off we went again, only this time to charter the boat to tourists in a land that was changing fast. Greece in 1974 was a different place. Tourism had happened, the car, electricity, the modern world was rushing in. Although still beautiful and fantastic the magic was fading.

It was not our secret garden any more, it had been discovered by others, the package holiday had been invented.

I was also growing and changing and in time would fly the nest. At the age of seventeen I became skipper of a 60 ft ketch travelling amongst the islands. I knew these seas well, but I was becoming increasingly nostalgic for my homeland. Here I was in Greece, but the book above my berth was Harvey Benham's *Down tops'l* about sailing barges and the marshes of East Anglia. So at eighteen I packed my bags and hitchhiked homeward across the Alps to a new life.

Bottom left & right: *Building boats at Perama and in the old harbour at Spetses.*

The barge Venture alongside at Maldon on the Blackwater Estuary, Essex.

FAVERSHAM

It was now the late 1970's and after some time bouncing around I washed up in Faversham, a fine place for wooden boats and still a stronghold for traditional sail with not a plastic boat anywhere to be seen.

Looking cheerful, Donald at the wheel of the Ironsides.

I quickly shipped aboard a Thames sailing barge called the *May* heading up to Scotland. The skipper was of the old school, with a dislike of idle hands. I slept in the hold, polished brass in the rain, and, as it was winter, was always chilled to the bone. I learnt to scull the punt and work the rig but this was not the life for me. I was too willful and headstrong to willingly take orders and had no intention of staying 'before the mast'.

Back on Iron Wharf in Faversham I wanted to get my teeth into traditional woodwork. My first proper job as shipwright was for barge master Alan Reekie rebuilding a Baltic trader that had lain derelict at the quay. She was floated into the dry dock as she needed new planking from the top down, a lot of reframing, deck beams and coamings, in all a big job. As Alan was away most of the time on his sprits'l barge, he put me under the wing of Donald Grover, a dour old so and so. Born in the 1920's, he started as a shipwright when horses pulled the timber into the yard and went on to work the barges under sail. Donald had a seemingly endless fund of stories.

We started at eight on dark East Coast mornings in a bitter North-Easter, called a 'lazy wind' as it does not bother going around you. We had a gas-burner on deck for tea. First

Sailing north to Scotland on the barge May 1979.

thing Donald said was 'Get the kettle on boy' and then, after stoking his pipe, he would start one of his stories. I worked hard in order to keep warm. Donald called this 'bosses weather' as the cold drove you on. At lunchtime Donald went off to get a pork pie, his bicycle always inexplicably getting no further than The Anchor. Several pints later he would return, 'Kettle on boy', then out with the pipe and a story. 'We was coming down Swin, tops'l set, it was . . . Let me see . . . nineteen fifty . . .' he would trail off, sucking his pipe in silence trying to remember the exact date. Then off again 'With Reg . . . no tell a lie, it was George Smyth . . .', again a long pause while he puffed on his pipe, then on he went with the story. 'No . . . t'was Reg' it seemed important that I should know exactly the 'who and the when' of it all.

As a lad in my late teens I loved his stories. For instance when as skipper of the sailing barge *Rowland*, he was swamped and driven ashore on Sheerness, or during the war years, when he was shot at by the British Navy for not heaving-to. 'Can't heave-to, she'll go over!' his skipper would cry, whilst sailing in over the anti submarine defences. 'That's the trick with a barge see, shallow enough to float on a wet sponge, but don't stop em or the rig al take her.' But best of all Donald knew his trade as a shipwright.

Above: *Two Thames barges built by Canns of Harwich,* May *(1891) and the newly rerigged* Beric *(1896) at the Southend Match 1980.*

Below: *A fine coasting barge, the* Marjory.

40

Before heading to The Anchor he would set me up. Many a time we would shape up a plank, thirty odd feet long by 2½ inches thick, staggering from the weight as we offered it up. After clamping the butt, Donald would stand back and with a knowing 'That'll fit' disappear off for his pork pie leaving me bewildered and still holding the far end. Determined to show him, I would have it all wrapped round and spiked in before he got back, when, without any acknowledgment, he murmured 'Kettle on boy' and settled down to stoke his pipe. It was a good arrangement for us both. For him it meant the job got done without too much effort on his part, and for me, I got to learn by being left alone. He would tell me how to do it and have no qualms about letting me know if I messed up.

Alan would return between barge trips to work with us. He was an inspiration to me. Alan had the strength of a bear and the bloody-mindedness of an East End boy. The man worked with all his might, nothing was too much for him. He taught me that there was no such thing as 'Can't do', just 'You're not trying hard enough.' We lugged great baulks of timber round the yard, jesting with one another. He would shout 'Get on with it, you bugger' as I struggled under the weight of a large oak trunk, pushing it along rollers through the massive cast iron saw driven by a long flapping belt from the tractor some thirty feet away. Sweating, we pushed and levered until a slab of oak fell off. Then back again for another run. I worked like a horse and loved it.

The Marjory *coming alongside at West Hoo Creek on the River Medway.*

Above: *The* Ena *alongside the* Felix. *The* Felix *was halfway through a sadly aborted rebuild and now lies abandoned in the marshes.*

Left: *Alan Reekie walking along the dry dock that holds the Baltic trader* Helga. *We have stripped back the planking to get a measure of the work ahead. The barge* Mirosa *lies beyond.*

Right: *Me at the age of 19 in the dock at Iron Wharf, Faversham, working on replanking the* Helga. *Life was mud, tar, bitter winds and living on the marshes in a railway wagon.*

Barges on the hard at Pin Mill on the River Orwell. In the front row are the Maid of Connaught *and the* Centaur *and behind is the* Phoenician. *I can't remember the others, but right at the back is* Hydrogen *as a cut-down motor barge still in trade.*

Once these baulks were sawn we lugged the planks across to the dock where they would be spiled and shaped to fit the hull. Wrapping the planking around cold, at 2½ inches thick, it took a lot to get them in, wedging and shoring off the walls of the dock as we went along. Alan, always pushing to get ahead, would come up with yet more ways to speed the process up. This time it was a hydraulic ram he had bought at an auction, 'This will push the buggers in.' With a flick of a button, and ten tons of pressure, the job was done!

So we mechanized, pushing the entire plank in with the ram, not the back-breaking wedging and working along until the whole plank was bent round the bluff bow, held in at a dozen points. However, the power was too easy to apply and made us blasé. On one particular day, having wrapped a plank around the bow and having it nicely set home in the stem rebate, the whole thing was held at one point by the ram. I drilled for the spikes and bent forward to blow wood dust from the holes just as the ram slipped. 'Whack,' like an enormous catapult, it picked me up and threw me twenty feet across the dock.

Alan just stood there 'What the fuck you faffing about at?'

Needless to say, it took me some time to come to my senses, blood pouring from my face. 'Come on lend a hand, back to it!' Afterwards I realized the only reason I wasn't dead was that luckily the moment the ram slipped I was only a few inches away from the plank. If I had been any further away the plank would have gathered momentum and taken my head off. To this day I have a scar to remind me that wood under tension is to be respected.

I grew strong with Alan's 'do anything' attitude, and his determination to take life by the horns has stood me in good stead. From Donald I learned the skills of a 'time served ship-wright' and from Alan how to bash it in and stop faffing around. Although I was learning all the time, it was said of me that I broke two things to make one. But I worked long hours for little money and lived simply in an old railway wagon, focusing entirely on the job, living and breathing it, my only recreation being the odd pint of an evening with Donald down at The Anchor.

After a couple of years I moved on, becoming a journeyman on the barges, moving about from job to job fitting new stems, timber heads, bottom planking, covering boards,

Right: Alan Reekie at the helm of his winning barge Ironsides.

Below: Maldon, where wooden boats still rule. The barge alongside is the Raven, with Edme on the blocks halfway through an 18 year rebuild.

rails, anything anywhere, always eager to absorb the knowledge of the men I worked with. Having worked with the massive timbers of these vessels there would be nothing to frighten me. The boats I built later were mere nippers of no consequence compared to these.

This was a boom time on the barges as a lot were coming out of trade and needed rerigging. Although this was the end of wooden cargo vessels in England it did mean that a good stock of well maintained wooden barges was available to rerig. The quays of Faversham were full of them, and as the sailing fleet was growing I felt that this world would last forever. Sometimes old barge-men and retired skippers would come down the quay to walk their dogs. One such, Charlie Reed, a small man, his hair combed back with brillcream, sucking on his pipe, said to me 'What you doing with that yacht then boy?' His attitude being that a barge cut down to trade under motor was still a barge, but out of trade, even if

she was as fully rigged, as on the day of her launch, was a 'bloody yacht, and of no good to man or beast.' A vessel working for its living has a special beauty of its own, but unfortunately times had changed. I could see Charlie's point, but for our generation this was as good as it got and I was right in the middle of it. I had found a sense of purpose in saving these vessels and thought that we could turn back time itself.

Any chance of my becoming a curmudgeonly old shipwright was prevented by the sudden death of my mother. This hurt

poet Leonard Cohen, for whom my father painted a whole series of murals around his house. Always immaculately dressed in linen suits, Leonard was a modest and generous man and a good friend and patron to my father.

Finding that I had a modest facility for the craft, and encouraged by my father, I decided to make a living as a 'pier head painter,' such as the painter Reuben Chappell, painting boat portraits and then selling them to their captains before the ship sailed. It seemed relatively simple and would allow me to become a nautical nomad, sailing where I pleased. There was one drawback. I needed a boat. Having no money rather frustrated my endeavours, but I was determined that so small a detail would not dampen my ambition.

badly. She was a good woman and a fine artist on the cusp of great things. My father had loved her deeply for 35 years and her death knocked the stuffing out of him. It was time for me to get back home to Greece and give him some support. So I packed my tools in an old van and set off back to sun, sea and . . . whatever it was that you couldn't find in the marshes.

I was now 21 and once back in Greece intended to do some badly needed work on my father's boat. Also I had always wanted to learn to paint with my mother, but now it was too late for that and so my father taught me instead, in the studio we set up together on the island of Hydra where he now lived. We turned his house into a place of learning and I became his apprentice. We worked well together. I learned the mechanics of painting and at the same time gave him the company he needed. A near neighbour was the singer and

Above: *The Dolphin Yard at Sittingbourne,
with the* Nelly Parker, *the* Oak, *the* Saxon,
the Celtic *and the* Anglia.

Right: *Barges alongside at Maldon.*

Facing page from top to bottom:
The Mermaid, *a beautiful barge built by Howards
(but alas she is no more), and the lovely old*
Gold Belt, *both houseboats at Conyer Creek in
1980. And at the same time in St Katherine Dock,
the* Convoy *and* Remerce *in the foreground,
and the* Olive May *and* Montreal *behind.*

Charmian off the Brittany coast after her rebuild, gaff rigged but still setting the old sails.

CHARMIAN

One day whilst working on my father's boat in the harbour of Porto Heli I happened on an old English cutter, derelict, but still afloat in the far bay. She had lain at anchor there for some five years, pumped out by a local fisherman, just kept afloat but no more.

Top: *A watercolour of what I thought* Charmian *might look like with a counter.*

A roost for gulls, she had become a haven for nesting birds. Thick with their droppings and trailing a mass of long weed, she sat there like a wild off-shore rock, her own ecosystem. Paint and varnish had long gone, the wood bleached silver by the sun, and the rudder, eaten by Teredo worm, had fallen off, yet incredibly, she was still afloat. Called *Charmian*, some say after the wife of Jack London, author of *Call of the Wild*, she was built in 1914 at Poole in Dorset on the lines of a fishing boat and sailed out to Greece by Sasha, a Californian surf hippy who had made money doing a surf advert for an American soft drink company in the late 1960s. After cruising the islands for a few years, he left *Charmian* at Porto Heli and returned to California.

This was the boat for me. I had fallen in love with her and she was everything in a boat that I wanted. She was old and full of history. I rowed out and climbed aboard to look around. Beneath the bird droppings, the mahogany panels in the saloon, the brass lamps and door fittings spoke of another age and quality. I was determined to save her. After several attempts to borrow money from friends I drew a blank. Seeing my plight, and not wanting *Charmian* to sink, a Frenchman named Jon Eve came up with the idea of commissioning me to paint fifty boat paintings for the £3000 it would take to buy the boat from Sasha. I was to sign a contract to paint the pictures to a certain standard and be finished within two years. This was a tall order, as I would have to earn money to live on and fix the boat, whilst finding the time to do the paintings. But I had no choice, and so I became the proud owner of a thirty-two foot bird's nest!

This was a good moment to acquire a boat as I had just begun a relationship with a French girl called Anouk, a delicate girl with a sweet temperament and a love of literature, and we needed a home. Once aboard, we began cleaning out all the junk. Everything had been left as if Sasha was returning the next day. Rusting tins in the cupboard gave us interesting meals – would it be steak and kidney or peaches tonight? All his old clothes provided a badly needed revamp to our wardrobe. Under the cockpit I found a crate with a pile of rusting engine parts, Sasha had obviously been halfway through a rebuild, but as no self-respecting sailor needs an engine I heaved the lot over the side. At the same time I pulled out all the electric wiring, ugly stuff that messes up the look of a good boat. We set to with the task of bringing *Charmian* back to life, finding old sails under piles of rusting shackles, and at the back of a cupboard old pulley blocks and lengths of rope. We could not get into the heads as yet, at least not until the young chicks flew their nest! Quickly the boat came together as we scraped and varnished the mast, sorted out the rig, and made a new rudder out of driftwood. It was make-do and mend, for with no money all we could do was patch her up as best we could.

Having fitted the rudder I naively thought she was now ready for sea. What I should have done was sail to the nearest port to get her hauled out of the water for the work needed to the bottom and the gaping seams in her topsides. Instead, I decided to sail some 300 miles to Turkey, fearful of paying any taxes due on a boat that had lain in harbour for so long. Off we went, across the Aegean to Kusadasi in Turkey where I had heard they had built a brand new harbour with a travel hoist. This was worth seeing as there was nothing like it in Greece. With good fortune and kind winds we made it there.

With *Charmian* hauled out I was pleasantly surprised at the condition of the hull. The bottom of her elm keel was badly eaten by Teredo, but this could be easily fixed by cutting out lumps and letting in new wood. The worm in the planking was only on the surface and could be killed by burning off and drying her out. The one thing that had saved *Charmian* was the copper sheathing covering her lower strakes. Curious to look behind the copper to get a good assessment of the hull, I stripped it away to find the planking beautifully sound. Oh what a mistake this was, and how it cost us dearly. Never ever remove the sheathing from an old boat – it's there for good reason.

Ashore in Kusadasi in Turkey. Anouk is hard at work burning off the hull.

Above: *Anouk aboard our proud little ship in Hydra harbour.*
Below left: *Sailing to Turkey with the awful rig she had acquired in the 1950s.* **Below right:** *Anouk is scraping varnish off the bowsprit.*

We had her all painted up and relaunched. Pleased with our work, I went below to put the kettle on only to find she was already half full of water and filling fast. Panicked, we set to with buckets. Even bailing like mad the water continued to rise. Rushing to the yard foreman I asked, in the most casual voice possible, if he possibly had a moment to bring over a fire pump. Ambling across to see what the problem was, he looked down the hatch where the water was now lapping the top of the chart table. Screaming madly in Turkish he ran off to rally his men. Soon a four-inch hose was down through the skylight and pumping with such force that I thought it would suck her innards out. Once empty the sound of the water rushing in through the seams was like Niagara Falls. I spent the next hour diving around the boat rubbing handfulls of sawdust into the seams. With this the leaks soon became a trickle and by the next morning had pretty much stopped. It had been hot on land and she had dried out too much, a lesson learnt.

Having her shipshape again our stay amongst these kind and friendly people was over. We set sail and cast off, away back to the Saronic Gulf and Hydra. We sailed down the Samos Straits and with a light northerly made good progress. As night fell the wind rose. With the wind came the return of the leaks. The sawdust was washing out of the seams. It was back to the pumps. As the seas worsened, the pumping became virtually continuous. We drove on westward, our course set for the north side of Ikaria, hoping that we could keep the inflow of water under control.

The wind was blowing hard and the old girl was under a lot of strain. Then, bang! The forestay went and the mast staggered. Quickly, we bore away to save the rig. We needed to find shelter fast. We sailed downwind to the south side of Fournoi where we hoped to see our way into a remote bay. I managed to fix the stay between bouts of pumping, while Anouk steered. We came upon the island with the moon low in the sky. It was a race to get to land before the night sky went black. We rounded the headland just as the moon dipped below the horizon.

The wind was screaming now and it had become so dark we could not tell if the silhouette of land was ten feet or ten miles away. Then a squall hit us, pushing the boat over onto her beam ends, the decks half under water. I ran to the mast to let go the halyards. As I struggled with the rope in the pitch black I heard the roaring of surf breaking on rocks somewhere in the blackness. We were done for, this was it! 'Bear away!' I shouted back to Anouk on the helm but in the screaming wind she could not hear me. I ran back. 'Bear away!' Anouk pulled the helm and, as I lent my weight to it, *Charmian* came around. With a crash of gear she gybed and over she went, the mast almost to the water. With sails half down and ropes trailing, we bore off in full flight into the night away from the unseen land. There was no way we could tack into a bay in so fierce a wind and total darkness, so on we went out to sea again, renewing our efforts at the pumps.

We drove along the south side of Ikaria, setting a course for Mykonos, which although 24 hours away, was about the

My painting of a Greek Perama trader.

only chance we now had for a safe haven. We continued to pump and with the coming of dawn the wind eased. Up came the sun, a ball of fire in the sky burning away the chill of the night and quickly drying our clothes. With the sun, the wind eased and the leaks abated to a tolerable level. We glided gently along through the morning, but as we came towards the western end of the island and out of the lee we could see that the northerly Meltemi wind was still blowing at full force beyond the island's shelter. There was an ominous line between the oily flat sea in which we were becalmed and the squally white caps of what was to come. Inexorably, we were drawn towards our next Etesian encounter with the gods.

Whoosh! Away she went, careering over the waves like a mad stallion with us hanging on for dear life. It was back to the pumps with a vengeance, uncertain if we could keep her afloat long enough to make Mykonos? All day we ran on and into the next night, to find ourselves again tacking into a bay with the wind screaming off the land. Again the moon was needed to see our way in and again it went black as we closed in on the land. Looking at the chart I found a wide sandy bay with two rocks right in the middle. I looked at the water now halfway up the bunks and knew we were losing the fight. We hadn't slept for well over 48 hours. *Charmian* was sinking under us.

Charmian's *deck, an oil painting by me.*

I decided to drive her headlong into the bay. If we were lucky we would run up the beach and if we were not then one of the rocks would have us – it was in the lap of the gods!

We stormed in at full tilt, unable to slow her in the screaming wind. In the blackness I could not tell if we were about to hit a cliff face, or run on, forever in open water. Then just at the

right moment a car came over a hill, down a track and along the water's edge, before disappearing. Fantastic – this gave me a fix on the land. Rounding up, the boat lost way and came to a rest, and I dropped the hook. With a sigh I looked around and to my surprise just in front of us I could see the phosphorescence of waves breaking on rocks. 'Heck! That was close, let's pump out and get some sleep.'

In the morning when I poked my head out the hatch the first thing I saw was a rock about a boat's length astern. Confused I went forward and saw the rock from last night about where we had dropped the anchor. We were anchored between the two. How we missed them I don't know, but a near miss is still a miss.

We stayed there for a day or so to try and staunch the leaks by diving under with a mallet and caulking iron. With the leaks much improved we went on. Both completely exhausted, we arrived off our home island of Hydra as the wind died with the setting sun. Creeping into the anchorage we sailed close into the beach before dropping the hook.

After making sure *Charmian* was safe we rowed ashore to meet our folks for a welcome home meal. Having wined and dined to our fill we walked back to the boat along a coastal path, happy to stretch our legs in the warm night air. There was no moon. Stars glittered in the sky overhead, as if a diamond-encrusted cloak lay over the bay.

Rowing out, I took my bearings as the boats at anchor lay hidden in the darkness. I rowed towards *Charmian's* position, then rowed some more – where was she – surely this was her position. I rowed around in circles, increasingly concerned. Had she been stolen? Had she sunk? I looked for a mast sticking out of the water. The sea around us lay deep, ink black, and still. Resting on the oars I strained my eyes, then around the headland far off came a water taxi breaking the silence and with it came a flashing light, piercing the darkness like a lighthouse. It threw its beam around the bay in an arc, catching things as it went, a fleeting shard of light. Way off out to sea, far beyond the headland, the strobe momentarily lit something small and white. 'What was that? . . . there . . . could it be?'

I put my weight to the oars. Faintly out of the gloom came the reassuring silhouette of a boat. It was *Charmian*. She was hanging by her anchor to the very last rock before slipping out to sea. What had happened? It must have been one of those

Above: *The rebuild underway between tides in the creek at Brouage. The old stern is on the ground while the new takes shape.*
Below: *Planking is advancing well and* Charmian *is afloat, yet still some planks need to be fitted.*

strange summer katabatic winds that you get in Greece, winds that fall down the mountains in a great gust and just as quickly are gone.

Life continued like this for us, the boat trying to sink with us fighting to keep it afloat. Several times we thought we were doomed to perish at sea, yet somehow we survived until eventually our voyages bought us to Avignon in France. By this time Anouk was tired of sailing and sinking, enough was enough. She left the boat, and what is more left me!

Mourning Anouk's departure, I carried on in a wretched way, continuing to paint so as to honour the contract. Life in Provence suited me, so I was content to remain here a while. Finally the task was complete, the paintings were done. Over the years this enforced routine had helped improve my skill as an artist. I had even had a couple of exhibitions, but I was rather tired of the introspective nature of painting and wanted a break from it. I still had itchy feet, and the Atlantic sea was calling. It was time to move on.

The next leg was around Spain, through the Straits of Gibraltar, and up to the coast of Portugal to the Atlantic coast of France. By now I had found a new partner and crew. She was also French and called Nathalie – a chatty bubbly if a little mad but kind girl, a nurse from Avignon. She was looking for adventure and so shipped aboard. At first we had very little language between us but nothing makes you learn a language faster than sharing a life on the high seas, and my French quickly improved. Together we endured storms and near sinkings. We were washed up on rocks, and nearly run down by fishing boats. With no engine it proved to be hard work. Fierce head winds meant it took weeks to crawl just a few miles up the coast.

Finally, we ended up in one of those notorious Biscay Storms where the seas are breathtaking. I have a vivid memory of witnessing a deep-sea trawler struggle under the weight of mountainous seas that swept it from end to end, with just the wheelhouse standing above the boiling water. I wondered what we looked like to them – just a tiny thing in all this turmoil where sea and sky are as one. It was like living in a Turner painting.

Running before the wind with half the rig being swept before us, I noticed to my horror that the weather deck was lifting. The backstay chainplate had torn through the side and was picking up one of the deck beams, prising up a large section of the deck along with the sheer strake. Having used eight of my cat's lives in the Mediterranean I promised myself that if we survived this storm we would stop pushing onwards and put our efforts to rebuilding the old girl. She had done staggeringly well; nevertheless there was to be no more sailing until she was sound and seaworthy again. The Atlantic was a timely warning. It was time to stop for a bit, sharpen my chisels and put a few ideas into practice.

We sailed cautiously into the small port of Brouage, which lay up a muddy creek in Charente Maritime on the Biscay coast of France. This beautiful rural place, full of marshes and oyster beds, was reminiscent of my native Suffolk. Here we would stay until *Charmian* was new and ready to head out again. We crept up a muddy creek between withies, heading deeper into the marshes to where we could settle our tired old boat into a soft berth away from the storms. Here we found an old abandoned lock-keeper's cottage which after reroofing became a lovely first home on dry land.

The local people were welcoming and friendly. I got a job shipwrighting in a local boatyard building big wooden trawlers whilst Nathalie worked as a nurse in an old peoples home. Together we saved up the money necessary for the task ahead. We were helped by Gilles Botone, a young chap who was sympathetic to my plight. He ran the local boatyard and kindly let me have use of his tools and workshop. Finally we were ready to begin work.

Since as far back as I could remember I had drawn up plans for the perfect vessel, the boat to sail off over the horizon with. Over the years, with lots of redrawing, I had refined and improved this imaginary vessel, gaining a strong feel for her shape, fuelled by dreams of where I would sail her. So by the time I came to *Charmian* there was quite a portfolio of plans and ideas.

Now I had a boat, but how could I make her the right shape? I had always wanted a pilot cutter so this was my chance to make the boxy old *Charmian* into a butterfly. She needed more sheer, and in cutting out the ugly D-shaped transom and then spreading the frames I could lengthen the stern with a counter, something I had planned to do from the first day I saw her. With bulwarks, rigging channels, a longer bowsprit, and fiddled topmast she might make a convincing pilot cutter.

So pulling her up the mud bank stern first to get her out of the tide I set to with a chainsaw. It is amazing how quickly one

Left: Charmian *with her new rig and a proud new set of sails.*

Below: *At the helm coming out of L'Aven.*

Below: Charmian's *interior after the rebuild, with a pond yacht I made for my son Dylan.*

Sailing out of the harbour during the Brest festival in 1992.

can reduce a boat to matchwood. I cut away the deck from the companion way aft, chopped out the transom and stern frames, and then gutted her from end to end. In one day I had reduced the boat to a wreck. So began the long haul back. I started with a new stern post with more rake, reframing the back end and including horn timbers to support the new counter. Re-planking between tides was a bit tricky. More than once I had to tack a piece of ply over the gap while she floated! In time she came together. Despite being down by the head and over to one side, I managed to get her shape true and sweet.

In the mornings Nathalie would give me a lift on her way to hospital for the early shift, dropping me off when it was still dark. I sat on the bank, waiting for dawn to break, happy to look at *Charmian's* dark shape coming out of the night air, enthralled at what I was creating. My father offered to do decorative carving, on her stern and bow boards, in the style of the spritsail barges, which finished her off a treat. By the end she had gained 6 feet in length, making her 38 foot on deck. After eighteen months work she was a new boat with a

new rig but still the old sails. But she was ready to go and I was proud of what I had created. The ugly duckling was now a swan.

By this time Nathalie was pregnant. I remember saying 'It won't change a thing.' Oh, the optimism of youth! Finally we moved back onto *Charmian* from our cottage and made our farewells to a land and people that had been good to us for the last three years. With a baby son, Dylan, for company it was time to set sail for Cornwall, to a job and a new life among the English for Nathalie. It had been eight years since I first saw *Charmian* in that bay in Greece and nearly ten since I had last set foot in England.

We arrived in Cornwall during the spring of 1990, sailing *Charmian* up the twists and turns of the beautiful Helford River, passing oak woodland that sloped down to the water's edge, to the little hamlet of Gweek. It was the top of the tide, and we grounded just off the quay. It was raining; it always rains in Gweek at the top of the tide. Quite oblivious to the rain, faces surfaced from within the other boats to look at the new arrivals and kindly helped pull us into the quayside with a rusty tractor.

The festival of Douarnenez 1992, with Charmian *amongst the barges and smacks and Nathalie on the quay looking on.*

Little did I realise then how Gweek would feature in my life to come. We spent a year and a half there helping a friend convert a 60 foot Danish trawler, *Andrea Jensen*, into a convincing West Country ketch. A fine handsome vessel, as strong as an ox, oak on oak, she made a good sailor. It was a fine job to do and I was proud of how she looked by the end of it.

Gweek did take its toll though. After a couple of years Nathalie and I went our separate ways, but thankfully we've remained friends. Deciding to get away, I moved *Charmian* downriver and across the bay to a deep-water mooring off Falmouth. This meant I could use the boat more, sailing her to regattas and boat festivals. The timing was perfect. There was just beginning to be a long overdue resurgence of interest in traditional boats, particularly regional boats. *Classic Boat* magazine had only been out a few years, and the excellent French publication, *Chasse-Marée*, was organising boat festivals and promoting the new build of some fantastic traditional French vessels. The attitude towards traditional boats had changed. No longer were they seen as worn out, slow old timers. Classic gaff cutters were being restored to

race again in the prestigious Mediterranean circuits. There was a rebirth of interest in the gaff cutter rig. If it carried on we would soon be seeing new wooden gaffers being built!

1992 was the year of the first Brest Festival of the Sea and I was determined to get there, and to Douarnenez. The festival was to be the biggest gathering of traditional boats ever, and I was not going to miss it for the world. Sailing *Charmian* across the Channel with a crew of friends, still engineless, we arrived early to a warm welcome but still empty quays.

Soon the first boats arrived – from Russia, Poland, Denmark and Norway. From Sweden to Spain and from Ireland to Portugal, they all came. For me it was amazing to see so many intrepid souls gathered in one place, so many sailors with their tales of great voyages. There were Viking long boats, Irish hookers, brigs and barks, cutters and schooners. It was as if I had died and gone to heaven. And the sailing – oh the sailing! – what an amazing time we had. From dawn to dusk we charged around in *Charmian*, sailing into every corner, up every creek, round every boat.

Like overgrown schoolboys still believing they were pirates, we attacked any boat we could, showering them with water bombs and then making our escape through the moored boats, weaving madly in and out. With everything set, tops'l and flying jib, we charged headlong through the fleet, daring others to follow. Sailing like this in confined waters was pushing *Charmian* to the limit. The harbour was so full of boats that you could not see the water, yet we stormed through the middle, hurtling up to quays crowded with cheering onlookers, before turning with inches to spare to the gasps and applause of all.

Performing stunts was my friend and drinking partner Big Nick, a Faversham man, a gentle giant, always the life and soul of any party, a man who lived to travel and travelled to drink. Nick was always a jester and would jump off the boom onto the quay as the boat gybed past, then jump back aboard as I tacked up to the quay once more, the bowsprit sweeping past the crowd. When close-hauled and overtaking others he would leap from one mast to another. It was glorious flamboyant fun. We sailed the boat to her limits and beyond. Never before or since have I behaved so stupidly with such joy. These memories will stay with me to my dying day, the pinnacle of my existence afloat.

At night the boats rafted up ten deep. We gathered on one boat or another to celebrate all that had happened in the day, drinking our fill until dawn, only to be woken to shouts of 'you're drifting' after being mischievously cast off. So before even filling the kettle we had to make sail. Once we were away,

Charmian, *third from left, in a raft up at Brest in 1992.*

the excitement would start all over again. After two weeks of this our thirst was finally sated and we were able to sail home again, but grateful to the French for their amazing good-hearted hospitality and fantastic zest for life.

On my return to Falmouth life had changed. I was in a new relationship and it felt time to move on to pastures new. I had met Sara, a 22-year-old mother of two children, Oona and Harry. She was attractive, with something of the Irish in her, and strangely magnetic. She intended to go to university in Sussex to read psychology. I wanted to make a career as an artist, which meant moving to Brighton, a good place for such people as us. I also had to come to terms with the reality of selling *Charmian* as a way of settling financially with Nathalie. It was a horrible decision to make, one of the worst. I was as

one with *Charmian*, we were inseparable. I could not imagine life without her. I sailed *Charmian* to Shoreham, spending the winter preparing her for the spring market. She sold within two weeks of advertising to a good chap called Martin Jenkins from Southampton. It was a painful experience sailing with Martin and his friends to her new home before stepping ashore and turning my back on the boat that had been my everything for twelve years.

I was 22 when I first stepped aboard her in the Greek sunshine. Now it was 1994 and I was 34 and standing on a wet cold platform waiting for a train back to Brighton, alone and pained at what had happened. This was a wound that would take years to heal. *Charmian* had been my first love, and always would be.

Charmian racing at Douarnenez in 1992. Big Nick is forward of the shrouds. How young we all look!

Eve *at her best, with the bit between her teeth.*

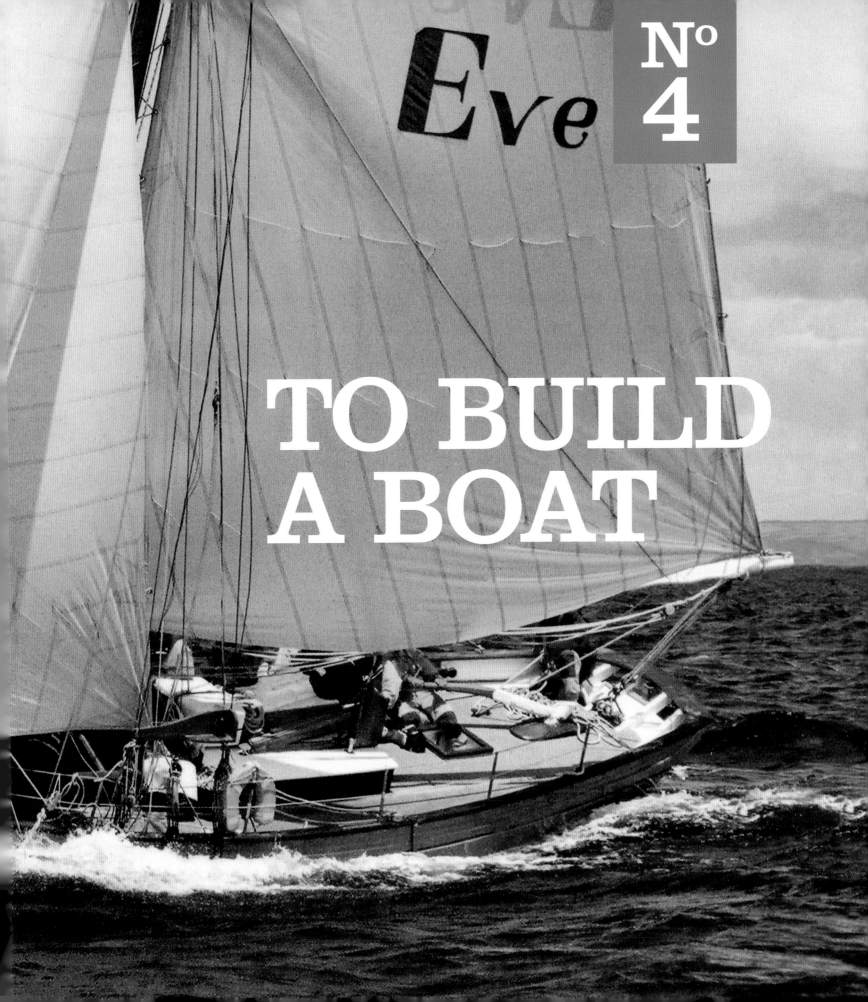

TO BUILD A BOAT

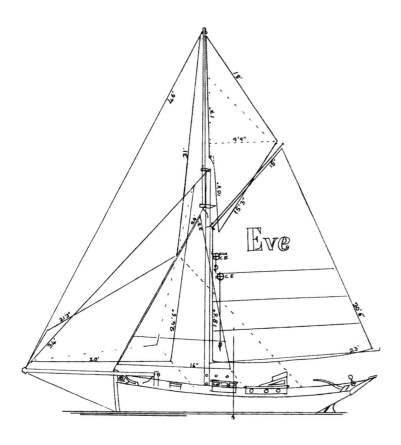

The party was over, it was time to grow up! I did not want to go back on the road as a journeyman shipwright. What I really wanted was to work on my own account, maybe now was my chance.

Top & facing page: Eve's *original sail plan and lines.*

By the time the dust had settled in the wake of selling *Charmian* and I had paid off Nathalie, taken Sara on holiday (and then split up with her), there was only £11,000 in my pocket. I now had to decide what to do next. Homeless, in a flux between relationships, this wasn't enough to buy into bricks and mortar – or anything else for that matter.

This future had to be connected in some way to wood. Perhaps a timber yard? No, that meant a muddy field dragging logs around with a digger, a container for an office, days on the phone buying and selling: no, not for me. Making things is what I'm about, a pile of wood that can be turned into something. The obvious choice was a boat. Selling *Charmian* had taught me there was a market for pilot cutters; yet getting hold of an old boat to rebuild did not make economic sense. The purchase of a hull was a foolish use of money. It would mean throwing away most of what one had bought in order to replace it with new wood, thus doubling the cost. Even when rebuilt it would still be an old boat – just fixed up. As with *Charmian* the sale price never reflected the true cost of the rebuild. Finally I reached the obvious decision – to build a new boat.

For years I had been watching the demise of wooden boats, seeing them being broken up, burnt or sunk. Hardly anyone was building new wooden fishing boats and no one had built traditional plank-on-frame yachts for many years. The numbers of these vessels were in sharp decline, a situation not helped by the EU Fisheries Policy insisting that fishing boats should be cut up as part of their decommissioning.

Ignorant bureaucrats, unable to see beyond the ticking of boxes, have condemned good boats that might have enjoyed new lives doing something other than fishing. Someone had to stop this institutional vandalism.

Fixing old boats is good but not enough for me, as it does not add to the ranks. The only way to reverse this process was for someone to start making new boats. National attitudes were negative. No boatbuilder I spoke to believed that new plank-on-frame traditional wooden yachts would ever go down a slip again. Yet perhaps because of my experience in Greece and France watching new builds take shape as a

matter of course, I saw things differently. Looking beyond all this prejudice, finally I could use all that I had learnt and put my convictions into practice.

From the age of nine I had been making models of boats, drawing pictures and plans of my perfect vessel. So it felt only natural to build a boat, a replacement for *Charmian*. The exact type of vessel was decided when visiting friends in the Isles of Scilly. Looking through a junk shop I came across an old book about Scillonian pilot cutters. Here was my answer, to build one of these beautiful forgotten cutters. A pilot cutter is about the best traditional boat of its size.

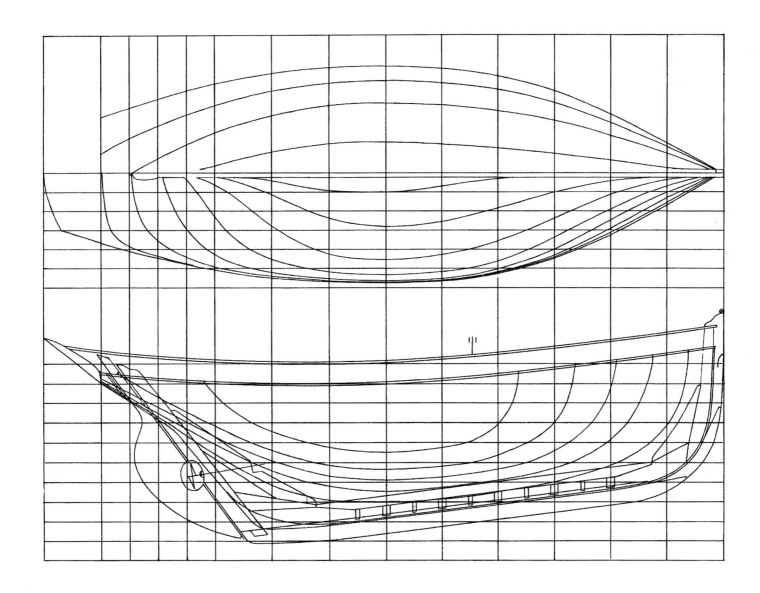

Fishing boats did not have enough headroom, luggers were not versatile enough, and cargo boats too big. Suddenly, I could see ahead. My mind raced, seeing myself building then selling this boat to buy another pile of wood, to build another and bigger again. Hopefully this investment would grow until one day I would build a boat of my own. But I was getting ahead of myself. One step at a time. This first boat had to be small, *Charmian* was 38 ft. My funds were meagre, and anything bigger than *Charmian* was impossible.

Having decided what to build I had to choose where to live. Getting out a map, I needed somewhere close to the sea or on a tidal river, and more importantly it had to be near my son Dylan in Totnes. My finger landed on Exeter, even though I didn't know a single person there. I left Shoreham in the summer of 1994 in a Ford Fiesta picked up at the local auction, packed with all that I had in my life – tools, books, clothes and a mattress. Once I'd found a flat and bought a table and chair from a local junk shop, it was time to set about drawing up some plans for the new boat, burning the midnight oil in my labours.

This was a strange time, especially as there was no-one to share the excitement, not even someone to go down to the pub for a pint. Despite this isolation I kept myself busy and positive. I have always loved the process of design, putting ideas on paper and watching the boat take shape. I may not be a naval architect but I know a good boat when I see one. If a Thames sailing barge can sail, and sail as well as

Above: *Jammed against the shed in Exeter, the planks start to go on. The steamed ribs will go in later.*

Below left: *Setting home the handmade copper nails.*

they do, then anything has a good chance of doing the same. Also I felt it important to work on paper, not a computer screen. The devil is in the detail, and no software I've seen can understand the subtleties of shape in a counter stern. One can tell at a glance if a boat has been designed on a computer. The curves don't follow the form. The result is a bit like a book being written by a committee – bland. Machines do not make Art!

Next, I needed to find somewhere to work. A farmer's barn seemed logical but even after asking around and phoning every farmer in the book I could not find what was needed. Then an idea – maybe the Maritime Museum would be interested in a working exhibit. Exeter's old docks were down-at-heel, but the Maritime Museum's historic boats and exhibits made it a fascinating place. Visiting the curator I wasted no time in trying to persuade him that having a traditional boat taking shape on one of their quays, would be a real asset. The response was sadly predictable. 'What do we need another pilot cutter for, we already have one?' Yes they did, but *Cariad* was lying derelict in a shed, planks hanging off. I was disappointed by their lack of imagination. How could anyone be blind to so obvious an opportunity to reinvigorate the Museum?

Dejected, I walked down to the other end of the docks. Amongst the old transit sheds was a ramshackle boatyard full of on-going projects, peoples' dreams, most of which seemed to be fishing boat conversions, forming a strange array of semi derelict wooden boats. I wandered in and chatted to the owner of the yard, Peter Jenner, an amiable soft-spoken man who seemed sympathetic to my ambitions. There and then he offered me a space. Finally I could get started!

It was time to telephone John Barchard, a shrewd and canny Yorkshireman who had spent a life in boat timbers and seen people like me come and go. He hailed from Hull, supplying the Scottish boatbuilding industry since the time of Christ. John knew pretty much all there is to know about boat timber and it was important to face up to his superior knowledge without being fleeced alive. Having already taken the scantlings off *Charmian* I had a good idea of the quantity

of wood needed, but it's always a bit of a guess. With not enough money to finish the boat, the thing was to get started and then I would find a way – the die would be cast and the rest would follow.

So John Barchard supplied the larch for the planking and the oak for the sawn frames and steamed ribs. As for the hardwood I had a bit of good fortune in that Malcolm

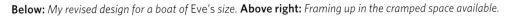

Below: *My revised design for a boat of* Eve's *size.* **Above right:** *Framing up in the cramped space available.*

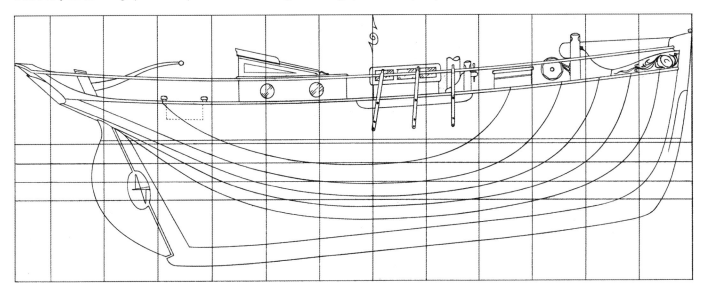

McKeand was in the process of rebuilding the pilot cutter *Kindly Light* at Gweek Quay and had some wood to spare. It felt good that my first boat contained wood from the same trees as this original pilot cutter. Next to decide on the fastenings. The debate was whether to go ferrous or non-ferrous. Whichever way one must be consistent, as dissimilar metals cause electrolysis. If I went for iron fastenings then it must be iron throughout, including the keel bolts. I considered bronze but as an alloy this breaks down in the end – even the best aluminum bronze will not last 80 years, in no way long enough for my boat! Not wanting the boat to fail because of its fastenings, in the end I chose copper. The Navy used copper bolts in the building of the *Victory*. If it was good enough for Nelson it was good enough for me.

Archaeologists will find the remains of one of these cutters in a thousand years from now and the fastenings will still be perfect! Copper is softer than other metals, so one must use a larger diameter. It is also a bit slippery in the wood, but as long as you clench the ends there's no problem. Its softness is useful as it can be cut to length, forged at one end, then once driven through the hull, easily clenched over a washer. Time and money is saved as there is no need for threading and nuts, yet it is just as strong. So I ordered copper round bar at seven-eighths of an inch for the dead-wood assembly and ½ inch for the deck beam, lodging knee and beam shelf, and for pinning the sawn frames together.

Above: *The hull finished and the bulkheads are going in.* **Below:** *Looking good,* Eve *is now ready for the deck planking.*

For the hull plank fastenings I found a load of ¼ inch square section copper (windings from an old electric motor) at the local scrapyard which I cut into lengths of 3½ inches and fashioned into boat-nails. Finally I bought some secondhand tools – an 18 inch planer-thicknesser, some clamps, a big slow drill and a circular saw: what more does a man need?

It was then down to physical work. The first job was to clear a site. I chose a quiet corner in the yard so as not to draw attention to myself; as yet I lacked confidence enough to parade publicly, feeling more like a misfit. In 1994 no one was building traditional wooden boats. The less I was noticed the better. The world is full of people who talk but achieve nothing. I wanted to be judged only once there was something to show.

The site was a bare patch of ground open to the weather except for the protection of a high stone wall on the north side. To the east were some disused transit sheds, and on the south lay an old boat under tarpaulins. I cleared a space 16 feet wide by 45 feet long. There was hardly enough room for the wood, let alone to build a boat. I would be outside come rain or shine, but where could the planer-thicknesser go? This was solved by knocking together a small shed out of old doors and corrugated iron which fitted snugly under the overhang of the counter stern when it was built. There was not an inch to spare. Doors on each side opened to allow the planks being thicknessed to pass through one end of the shed and out the other. Finally there remained a little space in the shed for a small bench. So this was to become my world for the next few years. From tiny acorns do mighty ships grow. Everything looked good. I was even back with Sara after our split-up in Brighton. She had switched from Brighton to Exeter University, bringing us back together again.

The timber arrived on a large flatbed lorry, which carefully backed into the yard, squeezing past the boats. With helping hands we levered the heavy baulks off, which crashed haphazardly to the ground. After this it took me a week with rollers and levers to tidy up, slowly managing to thread the wood into its allotted space. Eventually the piles were stacked to dry and placed in order of use, so that as the boat went up the pile went down, the longest lengths lying each side of where the keel would lay. Rolling up my sleeves and eager to get started, I first built a loft floor. In the little space available it had to be a small affair. Three sheets of 8 x 4 ply were laid on bearers. As it was November and winter was approaching I rigged a tarpaulin over the top. It felt like a

refugee camp cobbled together by children. On this floor I drew out the frames full size, cut templates from hardboard, then chopped out the oak sections with a chainsaw. I was totally wrapped up in the work, often arriving shortly after dawn and putting in a 12 hour day. Once all the oak pieces were cut, they were then thicknessed and assembled on the floor. Pinned through with ½ inch copper rod and clenched, one by one the frames took shape.

Next the keel; this had to be laid precariously on its side, balanced over the top of the stacks of timber. The stem and stern post were fitted and the dead wood structure assembled all on the horizontal. This allowed me to drive the seven-eighths inch copper bar through from the underside before clenching. Some of these were 4 feet long and proved too big to clench cold; so I devised a method for heating the ends with oxyacetylene. Shielding the wood from the flame and pouring water to stop it burning, once the copper glowed cherry red I worked madly in a cloud of steam, beating away till it formed a head. Finally a bucket of water to quench it all, then in cooling the whole thing tightened, squeezing out the bitumastic to become beautifully solid.

Craned out of the corner to a place where potential customers could see her.

Eve ready to launch, with Adam Purser proudly contemplating his command.

Getting the keel up was a great moment. After setting up sheer legs at each end with blocks and tackles we heaved away. People from the yard turned out to lend a hand as the whole thing had to be lifted high up before being slotted down into the gap between the stacks of timber. Like an Amish barn raising it proved to be quite a social event. Now I had a structure in the air, not just a pile of wood on the ground.

In order to gain more space I cut out all the deck beams and stacked them to one side. Next the frames could go up. This is the best stage in the building of a boat. Within a week or so the structure changes from two dimensional to three. Suddenly I had a vessel, only in skeleton, but you could see her shape and volume, sitting inside one can feel a great sense of pride. Now all I had to do was fill in the gaps – a mere trifle!

Working hard and long, through all weathers, not stopping for rain or snow; if one day was lost to bad weather then soon it would accumulate to months. I pushed on, often wet to the bone, or frozen, but still kept going. Eyebrows were raised in disbelief at what I had become. It did not help that I was caked in mud and tar, looking like a medieval peasant or mad man possessed. Having grown used to these working conditions from my time spent on the barges, working between tides in the mud, beating splattered tar-covered planks into place. On the East Coast we all looked like this, we were a community and proud of it, but down here I was out on my own. In Exeter people did not behave like this, they were clean indoor people.

The boat took shape and soon it was time to set up the sheer-strake. Not wanting to trust the plans alone, I needed to step back to see for myself. But as the boat was hemmed in on all sides, the only answer was to jack her up high enough to see her from over the wall. Then jumping on my bike and pedalling around to the far side of the river to get a good view and then back again to move the batten, a little higher, a little lower, until it was just right. Sheer in a boat is everything, it's what gives beauty and so must be perfect. Once happy with a fair line, she could be lowered back down and then on with the planking.

I carried on building until the wood ran out and still I needed the bottom planking, the deck planks, and the mast and spars. So it was back to Faversham to earn some money, several months away laying decks on other peoples' boats, until I'd saved enough for the next pile of wood. This done she was planked up. In went the shutter-planks. The starboard side was a bit tight, wedging and bashing I finally got it in to place and fastened before knocking away the props and wedges that had driven it home. I came to the last one. In the nick of time I noticed that the whole boat was picked up and supported on this solitary prop. All the other props that normally held her had fallen away during the tussle with the plank. About to be squashed, I stopped!

Once the deck was on, the lower mast in, and the main saloon fitted out, my lack of money caught up with me again and things came to a halt. Now was time to concentrate on selling the boat and finding a buyer – not an easy task with her half-finished. Borrowing enough money from friends to pay for an advert in *Classic Boat* magazine, we waited for a response. I assumed that my customer would be a hardened traditionalist, the sort of person that had owned a smack or spritsail barge, or had sailed the world with a pipe clenched between his teeth. Other shipwrights such as Peter Nash, a man who had also built new wooden boats, came by, full of praise for what I was trying to do and sympathetic to my ideas. But in the end there was little real interest and it seemed the potential customer was more likely to be someone seeking a lifestyle change, someone who had perhaps made money in the City.

When potential purchasers made enquiries they asked if the boat could be covered in epoxy or some sort of plastic, as they were not happy with the idea of wood as a safe

Below: *With* Eve *now sold, the crane has taken the weight while Adam holds the stern line.*

material in salt water. The problem was that new plastic yachts were being judged against old wooden boats. The newest wooden yachts tended to be at least 30 or 40 years old. People associated wood with work, often quoting the adage 'If you buy wood you are buying a problem.' On occasions I despaired. How could I single-handedly change attitudes that were now so entrenched? Those who most liked my boat were hardened sailors with no cash in their pockets. Those with the money had no experience of owning such a vessel. How could I build confidence in something with which they were totally unfamiliar?

In the meantime I fielded bizarre questions and did my best to defend myself. It was quite amazing the number of people who needed to tell me where I was going wrong. A whole year went by. There was still no buyer. I lowered the price as much as possible, even writing off a year's wages, just as long as I had enough to buy another pile of wood. I needed to get the boat onto the water and its sails up just to prove my credentials as a boatbuilder.

Then finally, after I had given up all hope, on the very same day, two offers fell through the letterbox. One, a gentleman wishing to use her as a houseboat for his son at Plymouth University, and the other from a couple who had met recently in the lazarette of a square-rigger, Adam and Debbie Purser. They were heady with passion and eager to set up a charter business. There was no competition. Here were my saviours. Now with money in hand, it was back to work and full steam

ahead to finish the boat. Finally, launch day arrived. People gathered, even someone from the local newspaper. Debbie smashed a bottle of champagne over her bow and named her *Eve of St Mawes. Eve*: three years of my life. What a moment it is when something you have worked so hard for is gently lowered into the water. This is the closest a man can come to giving birth! Quite unexpectedly a great wave of emotion swept over me, which I passed off as grit in my eye. She was made ready for sea; sails, fenders, ropes, lifejackets, and all. Off for a working life in charter that over the years has provided more valuable publicity for my work than I could possibly have imagined. On her maiden voyage we sailed her to Brixham and what a joy she was, skipping over the waves like a schoolgirl let out of class. I was happy, and more importantly Adam and Debbie were happy with their new command.

The paper work signed, Adam gave me a cheque for the final payment. My head spun from a feeling of release, it was over! I walked away, floating on air, his cheque burning a hole in my pocket. Within a few days *Eve* was off with her first charter party and I was back at the yard looking at the empty space where my first build had taken place.

What next? Whilst all this had been going on, friends told Sara not to let me build another boat: 'It would be madness to do so again. There's no market for new wooden boats. No one wants them. Sheer folly, it will be the ruin of you.' If I had managed to sell the boat it was a fluke and I should

count my lucky stars and promise not to do it again. But as Sara already knew, there was no going back. With the money left over after paying off all those we had borrowed from, it was time to pick up the phone and place an order for another pile of wood.

Facing page, far left: *Debbie Purser smashes the champagne on Eve's stem and names the good ship* Eve of St Mawes. **Middle:** Eve *takes to the water for the first time, what a sweet moment this is.*

This page left: *Friends such as Richard Sowman step aboard to help celebrate.* **Below:** Eve *leaving the Exeter Ship Canal and her first taste of seawater.*

Facing page top: *Adam at the helm with Martin Burton and myself behind. Away Eve goes like a schoolgirl let out of class.* **Bottom:** *Eve returning to her home base of St Mawes.*

Right: *Eve on her maiden voyage from the Exe to Brixham. The wind dropped as we approached.*

Below: *Newly at sea, Martin Burton takes to the mast with his camera.*

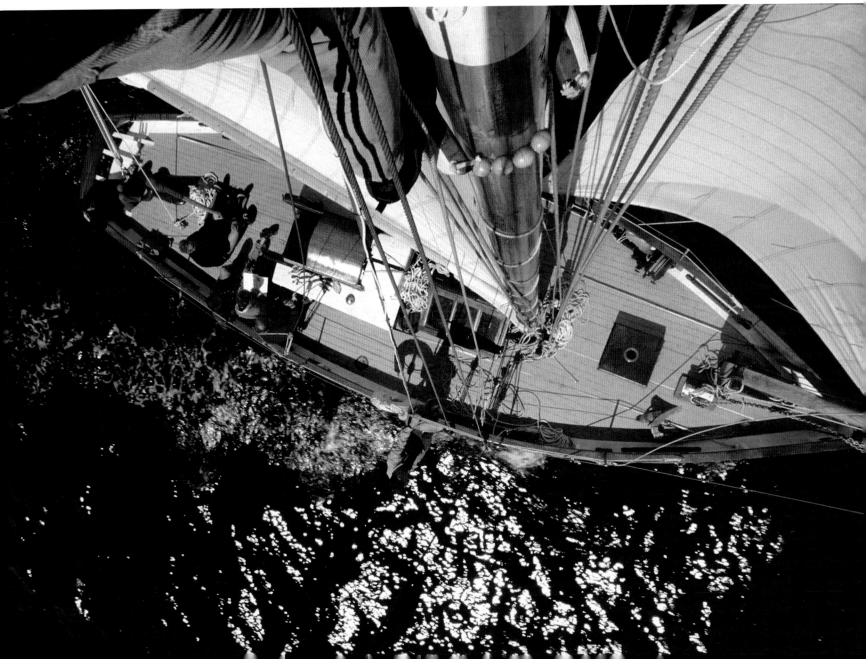

Reaching across the bay on her first sail. I sheet out while Arne steadies the helm.

LIZZIE MAY

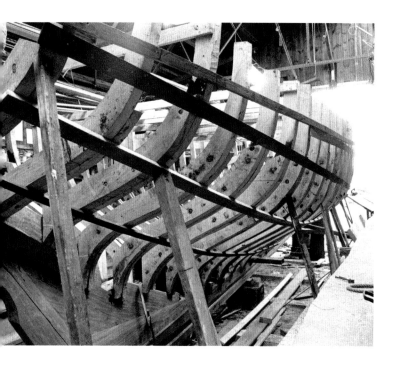

Framed up inside the shed at Exeter docks.

I set out my tools and painted a large sign for the front of the shed: 'Working Sail – Builder of Wooden Pilot Cutters.' Never again would I have to work for others. I was self employed and in charge of my own destiny.

Eve sailed away in the spring of 1997. To acquire the timber for the next build I had what I thought was a smart idea, sourcing my own oak in order to cut out the middleman. I placed an advert in the local paper. Replies came thick and fast as farmers all over Devon sensed the chance to pocket some easy money. 'Ere, I got a fine tree in far meadow, ooh fine tree ... worth a bob or two ...' The result was weeks wasted spent driving round some of the most remote corners of the county. Days negotiating rutted tracks riddled with potholes provided a fascinating tour of the secret life of old farming in Devon, but not much more.

One of these experiences was to a dairy farm down a long muddy lane which led to a crumbling Jacobean house and medieval barns under threadbare thatch. I waded across the slurry filled cobbled yard to a dilapidated stable door. The top half was held open with a pitchfork. A short stocky man in his sixties wearing a cloth cap and waistcoat, pushing cows into milking pens, looked up.

I told him who I was. 'I've come about the fallen oak?' 'Oooh ... Can't have that. Fine tree. You best see my brother ... in the house.'

Back across the yard to the house. I leaned through a dog-chewed oak doorway to see a near twin of his brother. He hurried me away, 'Don't let mother see. Come here sir, tis in the water meadow ... mother marn't know.'

Mother was feared by the brothers. She had never allowed either brother to marry for dread of losing them to the farm. In her late eighties, she still held sway and the purse strings, but the thought of a little pocket money had tempted the brothers. Walking down a waterlogged field we came to a bog. In the middle was a half sunk fallen tree. I couldn't even swim to it, let alone pull it out and cut it up. Promising to think about it I made my excuses and left. Maybe this was not the way forward after all.

Eventually, I found enough sound trees and, with help from friends, cut them into manageable lengths. Tractors then dragged them to the roadside, where a lorry collected them for the sawmill. Once sawn, they were brought to the boatyard and piled up ready for use. When I was finally ready to start chopping out frames, pulling the oak stacks apart, I discovered that they were all pretty much rotten. Hardly anything was worth using.

It was a lesson learned. Sourcing wood is an art in itself. My advice is to go straight to the sawmill. Talk to John Barchard and if the timber's no good you can always send it back. Timber yards can carry the loss of wasted timber as they mill such large quantities. It may cost more per cubic foot, but in the long run you have less wastage. Luckily, I had ordered sufficient timber from John to make a start. There were just enough oak-bends to do the framing. By the end of the summer, despite my failed efforts, the quay was again piled with precious timber.

For the centre line I chose a wood called opepe, a durable hardwood from West Africa, rather than the ekki used on *Eve*. Opepe is lighter and would also be good for the deck beams, coamings, deck planking, top strakes, and beam shelf. I wanted the whole boat above the water line to be hardwood, making her as durable as possible. The lower planking in larch would be fine, but you should never use larch for the top planks such as the sheer strake, as this is what's called a 'damp plank' due

to rainwater from the deck. Freshwater is a killer to wooden boats. With the covering board spiked down into a larch sheer strake, dampness will always soak in and rot will soon take hold.

Fishing boats built of larch, which have been solidly at sea for 50 years or more without a problem, once converted to yachts, soon go rotten if they lie idle in the rain. It's worse in the south west of England, as the warm wet climate is a perfect environment for rot spores. There's a lot of truth in the old adage 'Ships and men rot in port'. The cure is to keep them sailing and douse them in seawater or, better still, build boats from hardwoods in the first place.

This time, I was determined not to work outside in the mud and rain. The last few years had been gruelling. I had aged tenfold. With this in mind I rented half the neighbouring shed, first clearing it of old boats in various stages of decay, together with their spars, ropes, sails and piles of other jetsam.

Faring in the frames ready for the sheer strake. Lizzie May *is too big for the shed, so her bow protrudes from the doors.*

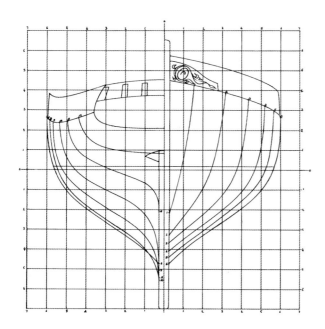

Guy Parker, who ran the shed, did all he could to help. It was a fine timber building with raised wooden floors, designed for loading goods wagons. Guy and I struck on the idea of cutting out some of the floor to make a well deck the length and breadth of the new vessel, thus allowing her to fit under the rafters and creating a raised floor around the boat. It was a world away from the one in which I had built *Eve.* Then I had been embarrassed at my working conditions, now I could take pride in them. I put in benches and set out my tools, hanging half models, plans and photos on the wall. I was in business, maybe it was now time to choose a name for the new company. I painted a large sign for the front of the shed, which announced 'Working Sail: Builder of Wooden Pilot Cutters.' Never again would I have to work for others. I was self employed and in charge of my own destiny.

Lizzie May's *empty hull looking clean and painted.*

Eve's old building space around the back became the wood store, with the planer staying in its shed. All the timber could be cut and planed out there, then walked around to the side door. The whole boat, apart from its keel, came in through this 2 x 6 ft door. Unfortunately, the building was 3 feet shorter than the boat on my drawing board, a problem I finally solved by making a v-shaped nose from scaffolding and corrugated iron to accommodate her bow. Leaving the double sliding doors ajar this cone fitted snugly between them. Passers-by must have thought I was making a missile silo or some sort of art installation called 'the Beak'!

I was now ready to start boat number two. As she was another speculative project, lacks of funds meant working alone again and marketing her once the hull was complete. She was to be 42 feet long – four feet longer than Eve – allowing her to be more aquiline. I needed her to be judged on her sailing abilities as much as her appearance, which meant she had to be lean as well as good looking.

I had sufficient confidence to decide that she should have a bigger rig with a longer topmast. The gaff rig was enjoying a real renaissance. Back in the 1970s gaff-rig was dead, seen only on the old timers. Performance boats had long since changed to the Marconi rig, but a new era had dawned and performance gaff was back. Great cutters were again racing, changing the way people thought. Now I wanted to do my bit to help promote the gaff cutter in the West Country.

Below & facing page top: *Lines for* Lizzie May *I redrew in 2010 ready for the build of* Freja*.*

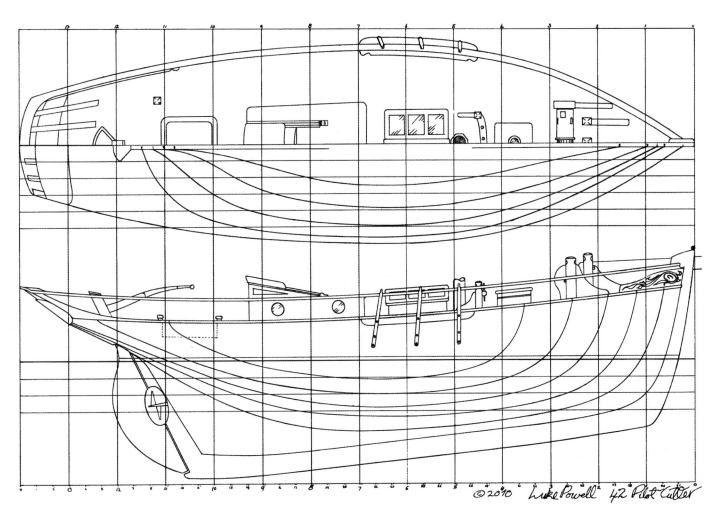

Sailing *Eve* taught me an enormous amount about the design of these boats. *Eve* had come out pretty well, considering how little I knew. Now I had a point of datum to work from and could iron out the imperfections. To this day I am still amazed at what a fine little ship *Eve* is. She may be dumpy with a short rig, but she remains a sweet hard working little girl. I've seen her sailing with snow on her decks. She works day in day out whatever the weather, a longer season than any other boats, and for this she deserves respect.

I decided to name the new vessel *Lizzie May* in tribute to the *Kathleen & May*, the last British-built deep water wooden sailing cargo ship still afloat. In my opinion, the *Kathleen & May* is as much a part of our heritage as the *Cutty Sark* or HMS *Victory*, yet few seemed concerned at her probable fate. It is only the tenacity of an individual that has saved her. Steve Clark has put everything he had into this vessel, despite being totally unsupported by the local council at her home port of Bideford.

At the time of building *Lizzie May*, the *Kathleen & May* was also being rebuilt. At 98 ft long and 136 tons this was a true act of faith. That she is still alive and a marvel to behold is due to Steve for his selfless funding of her restoration. The plight of our entire maritime heritage is in the hands of individuals. It is every man's duty to set to and build wooden boats - pick up your tools and get to work before wooden boats disappear for ever!

Lofting inside this dry shed was luxurious. With space to work I now had a system, having done all the head scratching with *Eve*. I felt in my element - this was my destiny, all that had happened before had led me to this point. I had a strong sense of *déjà vu*; it was as if I had already lived this life. Maybe I was connecting with my forefathers through the smell of sawdust and shavings. The piles of oak futtocks ready to assemble, the walls covered in shipwright's tools, augers, adzes, and half models - it all made sense.

In the rafters were spars, rope, and flax sails, and in the middle of it all, in the subdued light, a thing of beauty was taking shape. This was no plastics factory building 'Tupperware' boats. I am often asked to explain the difference between wood and plastic boats, to which I answer that a traditional wooden boat is alive with the voices of all those that have come before, she speaks to us as she sails. A wooden boat is a mortal creature - you talk to her and she responds. Walking through the woods, or along the riverbank, brings peace of mind, our worries wash away. It is the same with wooden boats. Unfortunately in this modern world the whispers of our souls are lost in the noise of traffic. Take to sea in a wooden boat my friends, and your soul will come alive.

I decided this time to go for all sawn frames after my experience with steamed ribs in *Eve*. As well as making the boat tougher, it felt a more authentic way of building, getting away from yachty techniques. As I set up the frames *Lizzie May* was

Below: *The wonderful* Garlandstone *at Morwellham Quay is my Mecca. She always gives me focus when the path is lost.*

Still in the shed, but now complete. This photo of Lizzie May *was taken to start the marketing process.*

becoming three dimensional, acquiring volume with her bow jutting out impressively through the double doors.

In planking her I decided to use bronze screws rather than the copper nails I had previously made for *Eve*. Although not as long lasting, they are accepted by the trade and easy to replace. The screws proved quick to use, especially once I adapted an old hand-brace to fit the electric drill. Whoosh and they were in, much quicker than spiking and setting home, and solid as a rock!

Planking *Lizzie May* proved to be surprisingly time consuming. The sheer strake and topsides were easy, giving form to the vessel. At first there was not much twist or turn in the planks but once I had worked down to the bilge and into the tuck under the counter the work became harder. One plank proved particularly obstinate. I had spent the whole day graunching it in. Heaving and clamping, taking it off again to adjust, I was determined to get it in place before knocking off. By eight

in the evening it was finally home, under a lot of tension, but there. Stepping back I was undecided as whether to leave it until the morning to settle down or fastening it before going home. What the heck, I thought, let's screw it up and start afresh in the morning. Picking up the drill to make the pilot holes I just touched the plank. One bite of the drill and bang! The plank shattered right across the grain. The day's work ruined, I sank to my knees in disbelief.

This taught me that when a plank is under particular tension leave it to settle for the night, or better still the weekend, before drilling and fastening. As the drill bit cuts the fibres of the wood it tears with a devastating consequence. If left alone the plank relaxes into place and will soon lose its tension. Because I was working inside I had another problem I hadn't had to deal with when building *Eve* – dust. The finest particles hung suspended in the air, and once settled formed a layer so thick you could write your name in it. Breathing it in was not healthy, especially the tropical hardwoods.

Lung cancer, one must emphasise, is a potential killer of boatbuilders.

During this period, if I ever found myself in a modern boatyard I became depressed at how different my world was. Theirs was a neat and tidy place of wall to wall concrete, the overpowering smell of solvents and resin, acrylic-boiler-suit clad workers, and everywhere white plastic. Luckily, I had an antidote, a place of refuge where I could go to worship the past. This was Morwhellham Quay at the top of the River Tamar, now an open-air museum. It had not changed in more than 150 years, a place where time had stood still. Alongside the quay lay the lovely little 76 ft trading ketch *Garlandstone*, built just down river at Calstock in 1909 by the venerable James Goss. She had spent most of her life sailing the Irish Sea but now was at rest in the sheltered waters of the Tamar. I used to go there in the evenings when the museum had closed and all was calm. I would sit in the master's cabin or stand at her wheel, listening and empathising with her sleeping state, wishing that one day she might again rise to the ocean swell and taste the sea air. Silently she would restore my courage and renew my belief in what I was doing, and I would return to *Lizzie May* with my vigour restored.

Once faired in the bare hull looked great. To show off the quality of the wood I picked out the top three strakes with varnish. Once sanded off the opepe decks looked smart, and with the coachroof finished, the companion way fitted, and the tiller in place it was time to get *Lizzie May* on the market. Photographs were taken and an advertisement placed in *Classic Boat*. I held my breath. Slowly enquiries started to come. The inevitable 'what will stop her leaking?' had to be politely answered. Questions like 'Why hasn't she got a cockpit?' were answered with 'The whole deck is a cockpit with these high bulwarks.'

A couple from land-locked Austria even took some off-cuts of planking and assembled them to represent a section of hull. Once home, they immersed it in a local lake to see what happened to timber in water and if my method of boatbuilding was really safe. From their worried looks when they came to the yard I knew the likely outcome. On went the marketing. Sometimes the callers thought me a kindred spirit and wasted hours explaining their techniques for anchoring. They seemed unable to comprehend that I was trying to sell my boat and had no wish to spend my evenings on the telephone discussing the finer points of anchor stowage!

With money running out, a friend called Helen who worked in a print-shop helped enormously by making up brochures.

Working late and without charging, she put together a bound colour leaflet containing plans and photographs. Once these were sent out, prospective purchasers started coming to inspect *Lizzie May*. But still I needed to get her to a stage where they could imagine her finished, which meant borrowing money from friends and running an overdraft.

One deal involving a syndicate fell through because *Lizzie May* was too small to give teenage kids a taste of Atlantic voyaging. The great sailor and redoubtable author of one of the Forewords Tom Cunliffe generously offered to do an article about the boat, in order to help our cause, but unfortunately at the last moment this was moved to a less relevant magazine. Carefully nursing the little money there was, I finished the metalwork, chain plates and belaying pins. Most of the interior was complete, yet significantly the back end lacked an engine, tanks, plumbing and electrics. There was no mast, spars or ballast keel. In debt far beyond what felt comfortable, and unable to afford the repayments on what I'd borrowed, I finally had to stop. It was time to get the boat out of the shed, empty the workshop, stop messing about, and get a job! So much for my determination to never work for others again.

This time there was no money for a crane. Making a cradle out of scrap metal and chopped up scaffold poles for rollers, and using a hand winch on a long wire, I laboriously began extracting *Lizzie May* from the shed. Slowly she emerged through the doors like a Trojan horse. Now I could finally step back to appreciate her true shape. She looked lovely, meriting a last ditched effort to sell her. Wanting to give the impression that her ballast keel was attached, I made a mock up out of ply and cardboard, which I then painted to blend with the hull.

More ads were placed in *Classic Boat*, costing more money I didn't have. Enquiries came in, brochures went out. The months rolled by. My hopes rose and fell like the tide. It was time for change. Things were afoot in Exeter docks. The council wanted to glaze over half of it as a shopping arcade, complete with cafes and shops. The rest would be flats and a promenade. In the dock itself, the scourge of all modern harbours, the plans showed a clutter of pontoons! The dock was to be filled right across with the accursed things – a parking lot for white plastic speedboats – this sad fate is being duplicated in old docks all around the coast.

Out went the Maritime Museum with it steam tugs, fishing smacks, and pilot cutter. Not to mention the wooden boats from Portugal, Italy, Indonesia, and China; beautiful boats patiently

OFF No 904523   REG TON 16⁴⁹/₁₀₀

Lizzie May's *comfortable saloon and practical galley, both finished in varnished wood and white panelling.*

collected over the past thirty years by the museum curator David Goddard. As well as the Museum, the council wanted to sweep away all the old industries that once had been the lifeblood of the docks: the machine shops, marine chandlers, boat repairers, boatyard – and me. Barely a working boatyard will be left once developers have turned them all into marinas and waterside apartments. In protest we gathered outside the council offices holding up placards and gathering signatures for a petition. To no avail. The council was unable to see beyond

Top: *Clive Emerson directs as* Lizzie May *is lowered into the water for the first time.* **Above:** *The christening ceremony with from left to right, me, Alf Jenkins ready with Star Castle wine, Arne Maynard, Sara, William Collinson – and not forgetting the boat behind.*

its collective narrow mindedness. I was told I could stay as long as there was no mess of wood and I made no noise. They planned to pave around me and glaze the side of my shed, so that from a raised platform tourists could watch me at work. I was to be an 'attraction', with an ice cream parlour for a neighbour. Needless to say I decided to move on.

So we were stuck, unable to sell *Lizzie* and feeling rather unwanted in Exeter. One day I was visited at the shed by Clive and Gillian Emerson of Gweek Quay Boatyard, who invited me to move to their yard. Clive, a larger than life character, was eager to make Gweek a centre for traditional boatbuilding. He saw good in me and I felt his goodwill to be genuine. At last we had a home for our business. Ironic that it was back to Gweek again, all roads must lead to Gweek! So the decision was an easy one. Sadly, *Lizzie May* had to stay behind, as firstly I had to set about earning some money. Clive was supportive and kind, despite his gruff exterior. Seeing my plight, he gave me a job on *Lutine*, the 60 foot ocean racer built for the marine insurers Lloyds of London in 1952. Clive had bought the derelict wreck and ambitiously set about a major project of restoration. I replanked her topsides, replacing deck beams and the coachroof. This kept the wolf from the door but was not enough to reduce my debts. I now had to learn to live with the broken dream of an unsold *Lizzie May* and a dismal future as an employee, no more would I be 'my own master'.

I looked at my rusting tools, remembering chisels and planes once bright with use. I wondered if I would ever build a boat again. Something had to happen! The only way out of debt was to sell *Lizzie May*. I dropped the price and renewed the adverts. When someone wanted to view the boat I now had to drive two hours to Exeter, pull the covers off, and look casual before covering her up again and setting out on the weary return journey to Gweek – thus losing a day when I should have been earning.

One chap came all the way from Germany. He sounded keen and knowledgeable, adding to my optimism as I uncovered *Lizzie May*, cleaned her down, and delivered my usual sales pitch. Gradually it dawned on me that he'd come to England, not to look at boats, but to hurry his pretty young PA back to the hotel.

At about this time a well-meaning Debbie, owner of *Eve*, published a letter in *Classic Boat*: 'Why don't people buy new pilot cutters? It's cheaper than fixing the old ones.' Her intention

Our friends gathered for the launch as Alf Jenkins gives a lovely speech on the pilots of the Isles of Scilly.

was to help me get a buyer, but instead it ignited a tinder box of indignation from a group of owners of old pilot cutters who had spent time and money restoring their fine vessels. In reply, a follow up letter stated that my boats weren't pilot cutters at all – to which a supportive Spaniard wrote in return that 'Luke's boats are just as real as any'. So on it went, back and forth for some months whilst I sat passively on the sideline bemused at the strength of emotion Debbie had stirred up.

What makes a pilot cutter? Owners of Bristol Channel pilot cutters should not feel threatened by new boats. Theirs are without doubt authentic originals, and my only wish was to help rebuild a fleet of what had become a dwindling boat-type. By enlarging the fleet with genuinely built replicas I hoped we could create a critical mass that might benefit all. Indirectly we could help each other. Since the growth of interest in new pilot cutters, all the originals have had a change of fortune as well, many being rebuilt. Maybe one has helped the other? Their

owners should not be wary of our new boats, or fearful that they dilute the status of the originals. Unfortunately England is a land of clubs, and clubs are about exclusion rather than inclusion. Maybe I was a rogue element, adding brashness to the fleet. If this was the argument, then I can only agree.

By this time *Lizzie May* had been out of the shed for a year and was starting to look a little weather beaten. It was October. Chances of a winter sale were minimal. By spring she would be shabby, look secondhand and half built. The latest wave of adverts had yielded nothing.

Then something happened. Several months later someone requested a viewing out of the blue. Going through the motions I did my bit, drove to the boat, uncovered her and cleaned her up. William and Arne arrived, down from London, William Collinson was a dentist in the City whose practice was fifty yards from the Bank of England and Arne Maynard a leading

garden designer (who incidentally in the year that I write this has won a Gold Medal at the Chelsea Flower Show). With a welcoming smile I showed them over *Lizzie May*, again giving my usual pitch. They liked what they saw, but I thought no more of it as I drove home. That evening William phoned to thank me. The next morning he called again, this time with questions. More calls followed. I held my breath, unable to believe that all the thousands of hours I'd spent building *Lizzie May* might finally prove to have been worth it. Then one day it was all over. William and Arne became her owners. It was back to work to get her finished. Out with the rusty tools, polish them with work and let the steam rise from the cutting edge!

The first thing to be done was to rent a shed at the yard in Gweek and move everything down from Exeter. Once that was done we were ready to fetch *Lizzie May*. She was craned onto a lorry, which then headed west along the motorway with us chasing anxiously after her. The lorry crossed into Cornwall, coming to a sudden halt at Goss Moor Bridge. The combined height of the boat and trailer was too great for the bridge. The only way forward was through a farmyard. Chickens scattered before this strange convoy, much to the farmer's consternation. With wheels on each verge we wound down narrow lanes until we found our way over a level-crossing and back onto the main road.

Top & above: Lizzie May *leaves the quay to start her life. We quietly motor away downriver with Esme in the foot well.*

Right: Lizzie May *takes to the sea with Jenny Bennett and Sara, Arne at the helm, Jonny Albrecht at the back and me at the rail.*

Lizzie May leaving the Helford on her maiden voyage.

It was Christmas, and with the boat safely chocked up in Gweek we were ready to start work in the New Year. I could put a fine turkey on the table at last. January 2001 saw us back in business. To speed things up I took on my first worker, Jonny Albrecht. He was young, keen and knowledgeable – sometimes too knowledgeable. He often exhausted me by questioning my decision making, arguing the theories behind form and function in boat design. But it was proof of his enthusiasm and we worked well together.

We had to get *Lizzie May* finished, rigged and sailing by April. We worked hard and soon the mast stood high and proud. Arriving at the yard Arne's face was ashen, he grinned nervously at the sheer height of it all, 'How will we handle such a beast?' 'Never fear,' I said reassuringly, 'It all shrinks once the boat's in the water.' William, on the other hand, driven by the

adrenalin of his new acquisition, was champing at the bit, eager to see her finished and put through her paces.

Launch day came and we decided to indulge in a little pomp and ceremony to celebrate the new birth. With a marquee, food, barrels of beer, and a traditional jazz band. *Lizzie May* was decked in flags and bunting. Amongst those who came I was delighted to see my mentor Basil Greenhill and his fellow maritime historian David McGregor. A group of friends from the Bristol Channel Pilot Cutters Association turned up to lend support and encouragement. I felt I had finally come of age after a long struggle. Best of all, our good old friend Alf Jenkins helped William and Arne in blessing *Lizzie May* with a bottle of Star Castle Red to the cheers of all. We had made it! *Lizzie May* took to the water. As she floated free from the strops, just as with *Eve*, a wave of emotion washed over me. To think she was

Above: *A fair wind from Alderney to Poole. William in command as we head for Lizzie May's home port. What a glorious sail this was.*
Left: *Alf Jenkins at the helm with rum in hand and about to strike up a song.*

Facing page: *The sail plan and a bird's eye view of us gathered aft as Lizzie May heads down wind towards Falmouth.*

finally finished, sitting pretty on the afternoon tide. I wiped the grit from my eyes. The beer tasted good – life was good. Clive came over and heartily slapped me on the back, 'Well done Luke, don't stop now, you're finally getting the hang of it.'

Next morning on the early tide, and with William and Arne on board their new boat, we slid down the Helford River; the channel twisting and turning through a still misty valley of oak woods, the engine gently purring as we tried not to disturb the peace. The river broadened, turned into open sea. As *Lizzie May* lifted on the first Atlantic swell I felt her come alive; she was flying her nest. With all sails set we tacked across the bay to Falmouth, going ashore to the Chain Locker for a celebratory beer.

The next day Alf Jenkins, our trusty veteran Scillonian sea dog, came down to the quay to experience the type of boat his grandfather had once worked in trade. We helped Alf aboard, cast off and set sail. Leaving St Antony's light to port we bore away on a beam reach. Settling down to her task, and with plenty of sea room, *Lizzie May* headed briskly towards the Dodman. Alf saw this as an opportune moment to bring out a bottle of rum. Apparently this was the necessary libation for such an occasion. The rum safely in hand, Alf broke into song. Not knowing the words, or having a voice to sing them with, I was a little bemused as what to do. The old Cornish have this tendency to burst into song at the slightest provocation. Us young ones have lost the art. Undeterred, Alf sang on, swept up by the memories provoked by these long Cornish ballads. With us sipping our rum and smiling happily, it felt good to have an old timer serenading this new boat, to be reminded of the connection *Lizzie May* had with the Isles of Scilly and their history.

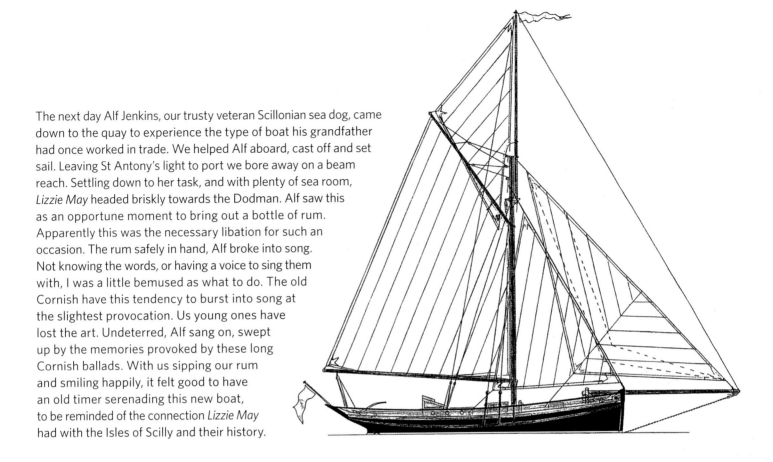

Agnes *sails into Falmouth on her maiden voyage.*

AGNES

You could sense the genius of the original builders who designed these pilot cutters, the knowledge that had been handed down through the generations.

I had started *Lizzie May* in the summer of 1997 and it had taken 20 months to build her. She had lain in mothballs for two years and did not sail away until the spring of 2001. The two dark years it had taken to sell her proved that there was virtually no market for new wooden boats. However, she did sell in the end. Even if it was going to take time to change attitudes I was determined to do so. Rather than being downhearted, I was oddly excited at the possibilities. The next boat would be bigger and better. I was eager to start work. This time I was solvent, with the freedom to make choices.

When as a young man I first visited the island of St Agnes in the Isles of Scilly, I had the strangest of feelings as if I was home at last, a deep connection. Maybe the isles do this to everyone, but I like to think this was a personal experience. So after going back and forth over many years I now felt it time to give something of myself back to the island.

Sara had decided to research the Scillonian pilot cutters as an MA in Maritime History, and thanks to her, my own knowledge had grown. In dusty archives and in the back rooms of museums we found old log books and photographs, few of which had ever see the light of day. It soon became obvious that much of what had been published was unreliable. It was wonderful to turn the pages of original logbooks and read the meticulous copperplate entries. At the museum on St Mary's there was, fantastically, an original builder's half model from the heyday of the cutters, the *A.Z.* (pronounced 'Ahzed'), built by the Stedefords in 1850. This model seemed rather neglected and unappreciated, stuck in a

Facing page: *The proud team; from left to right Will Stirling, Jonny Albrecht, me and Andy Cornish.*

Right: *Me amongst* Agnes' *timbers with her half model.*

corner, but to me it was the Holy Grail. Pleading my case, I was allowed to take the lines off this holy relic.

This now meant that I could accurately determine the true shape of a Scillonian pilot cutter. From it I would be able to extrapolate all I needed to recreate an exact copy of the *Agnes*, built in 1841 at the same yard. I had chosen the *Agnes* as she was the last cutter to work out of the isles and hailed from the island of St Agnes.

There were consequences to consider. If I built such a boat, her chunky shape, square forefoot, and square lute stern might make her difficult to sell. What the heck! I owed it to history and what's more I owed it to myself; if I didn't have a go then who would. I wanted to build a boat to a higher level of authenticity than any previously seen amongst pilot cutter look-a-likes. Although we only had one photo of her

at a distance and one of her at the quay half hidden behind other boats, we did have her registration document with the original size and tonnage, some photos of sister cutters and the plans I had drawn up of the *A.Z.*

Like bringing a dinosaur to life from DNA trapped in amber, I now had the DNA of a true pilot cutter. This was living history; the real thing! Although *Agnes* had been lengthened twice in her life, I decided to build her to the original size, as she was when first launched. This was the vessel I had wanted to build for as long as I could remember. She was finally on the drawing board.

Once I had established the boat's hull shape and deck layout, I studied the framing and structure of the hull. *Agnes* had a lute stern, a type not built since the 1850s. The only surviving example I knew about was a little Colne smack called *Mary*, who happened to be in a rebuild at the time in a yard at Maldon. I drove up from Cornwall to Essex, but unfortunately the *Mary's* stern was different to that of a larger pilot cutter and the journey was largely wasted. More useful were the models held at the Science Museum in London and engravings by naval architects of revenue cutters from the 1790s to the 1820s. The Navy were good at documenting construction details, so through them I gained an understanding of the framing structure of this long forgotten shape.

As with the stern, so also the bow. The square shape of the forefoot was old-fashioned and unfamiliar to the modern eye. Doubters voiced their concerns, saying that she would not round up and tack with such a grip on the water for'ward, and that the narrow rudder of her period would provide insufficient bight on the water to turn so long keeled a boat.

It was difficult sticking to one's guns. Even a well known naval architect questioned my sanity. To build a shape that was long extinct and, in his mind, wisely superseded, was folly. Yet from the lines I could see a sweetness of form, whilst the old log books, some spanning thirty years or more, were proof that these vessels had survived weather that would have kept many modern yachts firmly in harbour. In the end *Agnes* has proved to be a beautiful sailor and tacks with confidence.

Left: *Chopping out* Agnes's *frames, shaped and on the lofting floor.*

Facing page: *Frames and wood everywhere. Once the centre line is raised and in place the frames are soon set up, giving volume to the boat.*

In a weak moment I added 4 inches to the rudder blade, but after the first year sailing this proved quite unnecessary and was removed.

But before *Agnes* could put to sea she first had to be built. One day in the autumn of 2001 three lorries laden with timber arrived at Gweek. With the yard crane and forklift we moved much of it into the shed. The rest we piled wherever there was a spare corner, much to Clive's consternation. A wry smile was the usual outcome. We scattered the oak bends at the front of the shed, spread about like a pack of playing cards, ready for the selection process.

The next task was to put the timber 'in to stick' by placing battens between each board to allow the wind to blow through. With the high stacks of opepe this was heavy work, achieved using jacks and wedges driven in with a maul to prise a gap for the battens. After a weary week of hard work it felt good to see all the timber set up and drying.

The lofting floor was laid out above the stacks of timber some three feet from the ground, something like a dance floor. I looked like a crazed performer on stage, on view to the world. I set to, drawing out in full size the lines of the new boat. First lofting out the waterlines, from amidships to stern, then amidships to bow, half the boat at a time. Then the breadth moulds took shape, cross-referencing all the time, ironing out the flaws in the drawings.

Once happy with the fairness of the lines, I cut out the templates, carried them over to the slabs of oak strewn about the yard, and began ferreting through the pile for the best slab for each of the shaped templates. After chalking the outline of the template onto each piece of oak I set to with the chainsaw. After two weeks there was a large pile of numbered bits, like pieces of some strange jigsaw puzzle stacked high and drying in the wind.

They then had to be thicknessed, shaped and bevelled accurate to the breadth drawings, and assembled on the lofting floor. Once this was done, they were pinned together

Left: *Me drilling for keel bolts.*

Facing page: *Assembling the stern. The structure of the lute stern took some research to produce, first on paper and then in wood.*

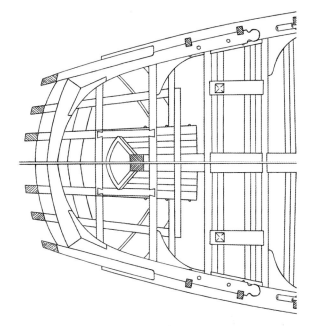

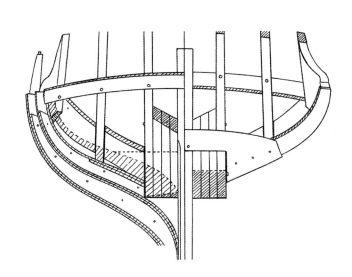

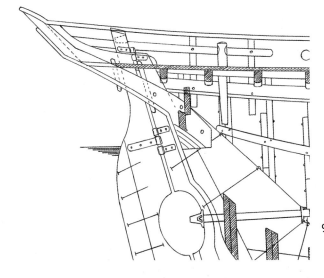

with ½ inch copper rod. I had learned from the previous boats that it was unnecessary to hold the assembled frames together by clenching the rod each side, blind dumps were sufficient, as once the planks were wrapped around her, the frames were going nowhere. Quickly these frames took shape and were stacked wherever I could find space – upside down, leaning this way and that. Jonny was still in the yard and glad to lend a hand moving the frames.

I worked happily in my own space, carefree and pleased with what was coming to life before my eyes. Six years after starting on *Eve*, I was finally building an authentic replica of an actual pilot cutter that had existed in 1841, a museum standard genuine working boat. Whether people would appreciate her was another matter.

The world was changing. The internet had come of age. The concept of a website made the potential for worldwide marketing a possibility. We had to get online to market the boat. Having made several attempts at this, using friends to build something on the cheap, it soon became apparent that proper money needed to be spent. With the help of a small

grant and Christian Topf Design in Falmouth the Working Sail website was born. We also switched to digital cameras, vastly improving our photographs. A modern man moving with the times! Maybe not – I was still two years away from accepting mobile phones, preferring to stand in the local telephone box with a fistful of coins to make business calls. But the website looked good and we immediately started getting feedback from interested people.

Soon we had an American wanting to come over to see the boat. By the end of winter and with spring just around the corner I began the process of planking, working down from the sheer strake with opepe, before changing to larch after the top three strakes.

Lizzie May was back in the yard for her winter refit and came out of the shed fresh from a makeover, a big shiny paint job that made her hull look like glass. William and Arne were planning a long season and wanted her launched as early as possible. I would come to work on cold February mornings to see *Lizzie May* standing proud beside my shed in the morning frost with Jonny rerigging her. It was good to have the two

Below left & right: *Andy and me planking up* Agnes. *The first half was planked from the sheerstrake down.*

boats together, *Lizzie May* ready for sea and *Agnes* taking shape. ***Eve*** had also spent the winter in the Gweek yard, so it seemed as if I was surrounded by the fruits of my labour.

Lizzie May was to be craned in on the coming Saturday for the early morning tide. I had not been involved with the refit as Jonny had dealt directly with William and Arne, but in a rash moment I had promised to help with the craning. Friday night was drinks night. When the alarm went off at five in the morning, all I could do was to turn over and nurse my hangover.

At seven the phone rang. 'Hello. It's William, they've smashed her.' 'What do you mean smashed her?' 'The crane dropped *Lizzie May*, fell on top of her, she's chopped in half.'

Quickly I struggled into my jeans and rushed out of the house. I drove the eight miles to the yard with my head full of images of my sweet *Lizzie May* smashed to pieces, spewed open, the hull cut down to the keel, all those years of work gone, destroyed. How could they do it! I arrived at the scene of the accident to a throng of onlookers and general mayhem.

Pushing through the crowd I came to an ashen-faced William in a state of shock, his lovely boat dead.

With dread I moved forward to see what had happened. *Lizzie* lay eschew in the cradle with the crane's jib wrapped over the top of her. Frayed wire and shards of wood were everywhere. The jib had cut through the gaff and boom, the rigging smashed. The mast was bent aft, sprung back with the weight on the after shrouds. The skylight and coachroof were punched in and the bulwarks had been demolished, but the thing I feared most had not happened, the planking of the hull, the sheer strake and covering board had held.

The crane's lattice jib had buckled and wrapped itself over the boat but had not sliced the hull in two; even so, it was a depressing sight. There was splintered wood everywhere. It was as if an explosion had taken place. How no one had been killed I don't know. The topmast had been sheared off with the initial shock and had buried itself two feet into the ground beside the boat.

The cradle was bent where *Lizzie* had fallen back into it. She had also spewed her seams midships where the impact had

The second half was then closed from the garboards up. Andy is drilling for fastenings while I clamp in place the second to last shutter plank.

Left: *Andy stands between the deck beams, about to fit the king plank.*

Facing page: *Andy inside the empty hull fitting the compression posts.*

taken place; two planks under her bilge were punched out where the compression posts at the bridge deck had been driven down and all her deck beams were broken from mast to tiller. Even the heel of the bowsprit, 9 inch thick Douglas fir and drawn back past the mast, had been karate chopped clean through.

Lizzie May had been about four feet up when the wire that held the crane's jib parted. It now lay snaked over the ground, the end frayed like a piece of wool from the flailing it had done, whipping back and forth through the pulley blocks. It was sheer chance that someone had not been decapitated. The crane's hook, steel spreaders and chains, all weighing a ton or more, had miraculously fallen beyond the boat. The top end of the jib, as it folded over *Lizzie May*, had also demolished the wheelhouse of the next boat and damaged the one beyond that.

I stood back in shock and looked at Rick the crane driver. He was badly shaken and lucky to be alive. Clive was also

grey, but managed to mobilise the yard-hands into tidying up. The marine surveyor arrived and another crane came. Next they started taking a chainsaw to Lizzie's mast. I had to leave, this was too much. It was one thing seeing the boat smashed, quite another watching her being laid into with chainsaws.

With William and Arne, Sara and I walked away down the yard, tears streaming from our eyes at what had happened. It felt like a death in the family. We were dazed. There was no boat, no sailing to be done, and no joy. What would happen to *Lizzie May*? She was tidied up and put in the corner of the yard, hidden away, covered with tarpaulins. She was to remain like that for years while all the legal stuff was sorted out. This was a major setback. I had lost a boat and we were now back to only *Eve* on the water.

William and Arne were understandably distraught at the loss of their boat. Unaware that we had a potential customer coming over from America, they deliberated about the idea of buying *Agnes*. But I felt she was too stocky and too much like a workboat for them. After *Lizzie May* they needed something with more elegance. In the end I promised them that the next boat on the stocks would be a replacement for *Lizzie May*, which would mean them having a two-year wait before getting back on the water.

In due course our American arrived. Shel Wappler was full of American gusto, wowed by all he saw. A tall urbane man from an old establishment New England family, he was my age and looking for a change of life. I liked him and sympathized with his quest. We even discovered a mutual connection through Peter Throckmorton and the Greek schooner *Stormy Seas*. He was delighted by what he saw, and loved the boat even though she was only in frame. 'Yes, gee, I'll have her,' he said, then, as quickly, jumped on a plane back to the U.S. That was easy. We had not even tried to sell the boat, things had changed! With *Agnes* sold and a commission to replace *Lizzie May* our fortunes had changed.

Maybe the sailing fraternity was finally starting to take notice of what I was doing, gaining confidence in the boats I was building. Maybe we were out of the dark times and *Lizzie May's* accident was not going to scupper things. Maybe my chosen path was going to work after all. Ok, let's get *Agnes* built and on to the next one as soon as possible.

With the owner's money in the bank at this early stage of the build I could gather a workforce to speed things up. First to join was Andy Cornish, a good man with a happy disposition who knew shipwrighting like the back of his hand. Of my generation, just a couple of years younger, he slotted in immediately. Working together on the planking was a pleasure. In tune, we understood each other's ways, joking and jesting in our labours.

Then Jonny back from his travels came aboard, getting the decking sorted. Once this was laid I took on Grant, a New Zealander, to help with the internal joinery. This was a good team and it was a great feeling to see the vessel progressing in so many places simultaneously. The level of industry was

Rigged and ready to go, there is no better sight than a new wooden boat.

energising. Everywhere I looked, things were happening and even if I stopped, the progress continued. For me the change from one pair of hands to many after the years of struggle was a totally wondrous experience. Never before had I been in this situation, not just running my own show, but with a good band of followers. We were a force, we could change the world and we were going to damned well try.

We worked hard and played hard. Come Friday evening we washed away the week's toil and celebrated life to the full. Straight from work, still covered in tar and paint, we headed for the pub. By closing time we were often rolling around the floor – much to the bemusement of the other customers. This was as good as it gets.

Agnes came together quickly. You could sense the genius of the original builders who designed these pilot cutters, the knowledge that had been handed down through the generations until her shape and lines had been perfected. She was so easy to plank, even without steaming, they fell into place.

Three months had her planking wrapped up. Six months from laying the keel to laying the deck. Although *Agnes* had been sold I still thought of her as mine. If ever there was a boat with my name on it this was the one, hence I think my willingness to risk building such a big boat as a speculative project. I would have been quite happy to keep her, apart, of course, from the small issue of not having the means to foot the cost of the build.

With the hull complete we began the fit out. It was time to take on another worker. Will Stirling joined the team. He was a young lad who had naively bicycled all the way from Northumberland on an old boneshaker and although not a boatbuilder his eagerness to help was persuasive. I did not have the heart to turn him away, so put him to painting. The amount of painting to be done on any new boat is immense and easily overlooked. It took Will months to catch up with sanding and painting all the woodwork the rest of us were producing. Once all the external work was finished it was time to get *Agnes* out of the shed and start on the rig. Also we needed the shed space for the next build, the replacement for *Lizzie May*.

William and Arne wanted to get her started as quickly as possible. Overlapping the builds meant that as *Agnes's* woodwork was finished, Andy and I could transfer to the new build leaving Jonny, Grant and Will to finish *Agnes*. As things progressed and *Agnes* wound down, all would be able to move to the next boat. This worked well, giving a seamless transition from one to the other.

Left: *Viewed from behind one sees the clean run to* Agnes's *hull.*

Right: *Down below all is brightly finished and on the foredeck the obligatory barrel windlass looking most purposeful.*

Our good American Shel returned to see *Agnes*. He arrived on a bitterly cold winter's day just after the mast had gone in. He was with us for about half an hour. 'Gee. Great! Keep it going boys,' he said, heading off to a wine bar. Having eagerly awaited Shel's reaction to our labours, and a little perplexed at his almost casual indifference, we shrugged our shoulders and carried on, knowing that even if the owner did not realise it, we had built one heck of a boat.

Launch day dawned. We were into the final stage. Deciding to celebrate as best we could, we sent out printed invitations, extending an open welcome to all the folks from the Isles of Scilly. We wanted to make a good splash with food and drinks and a jazz band. This time, after our previous disaster with the crane, we decided to have *Agnes* in the water and ready to sail away at the end of the proceedings on the rising tide. I was pleased to see faces from the Islands; a good turn out of Scillonians who had made the effort to come over in support of the rebirth of *Agnes*. Alf Jenkins, though now an old man and somewhat frail, steadied himself with his stick and read a great speech telling much of his history in the Isles and his family's involvement with the original *Agnes*. John Nicholls, the current pilot of the Islands read the 'Pilots Psalm'. Shel spoke some good words on the future of *Agnes* in America. We all hugged while *Agnes* looked on, a connection with the past and the future. Time came to cast off and away down the river to her new life. Everyone waved from the quay, many with a damp eye.

We thrashed *Agnes* through her sea trials. The first day out it was gusting, 'force frightening'. She lay over to the wind, lee decks awash. Under ballasted, she was light and went over on her beam ends, a good taste of the salty sea. Brad Cain, the rigger, stood on the lee rail immersed up to his waist bellowing for joy. I shouted back in delight and Shel looked on in disbelief, 'God damn, these are salty fuckers!'

A little more lead ballast was needed before we headed out next, on this occasion to Looe Luggers Regatta. Looe is always a great party, but it was also good for me to see *Agnes* sail amongst the other boats to get the full measure of her. She proved herself fast and showed great potential. Next the obligatory and much anticipated pilgrimage back to the Scillies to take *Agnes* home to where she belonged. We had to show her to all those who had supported us in our quest to build this good ship. It was a poignant moment mooring her where the original *Agnes* lay some hundred and forty years before.

Above: *Out on the boom reeving one of the reefing pennants, Shel Wappler getting to grips with his new boat.*

Facing page: *Putting* Agnes *through her paces on her sea trials in Falmouth Bay.*

The time came for *Agnes* to sail away across the Atlantic to America. She was piled high with stores. Every locker and cupboard was crammed with sacks of potatoes and mountains of tins for the weeks she would spend at sea. The delivery crew was aboard and ready even for an Arctic expedition! Skippered by Chris Rees, a fine deep-sea sailor, our own Jonny went as first mate. This reassured me, as he knew the boat only too well. Two young lads made up the remainder of the crew. Shel shipped aboard, a little nervous at the voyage they were about to embark on. Away, out of Falmouth harbour they went – away out of our lives. *Agnes* meant a lot to me. We had given so much to her and she had given as much back, yet this was not a time for sentiment. After all we can always build another boat. Even so I was saddened to think that this would be the last time I would ever see this fine vessel. I shrugged my shoulders and turned my back on the sea. It was time to return to the yard and to the next boat.

A blustery day with an Atlantic swell running as Hesper passes the Fastnet rock.

HESPER

Personally, my own needs are simple. All I want is to be left in peace in a secluded valley with a good woman and a boat to build.

Above: *Little Esme wants to join in, as we assemble one of* Hesper's *bow frames.* **Top right:** *Cutting out the frames for* Hesper *with the soon-to-be-completed* Agnes *behind.*

Facing page: *On the second day out with* Hesper *we lost the wind but the sun shone brightly.*

When the news of *Lizzie May's* accident spread the inevitable sharks surfaced, smelling the opportunity of a deal, the possible chance to sell William and Arne a replacement boat. Attempts were made to seduce them away from us by enticements of restoring a Bristol Channel pilot cutter or finished vessels of equally noteworthy pedigree.

It was imperative that William and Arne came back to me for their next boat, otherwise it would be a bad indictment on my reputation as a boatbuilder. After losing their boat I could not lose them as well. To their credit they stayed with us, despite the lures of others and the fact that they would have to wait a year or more for me to finish *Agnes*. Working with William, we thrashed out what would be a good arrangement for their next vessel.

We agreed to strip anything of value from *Lizzie May* in order to equip the new boat, after which I would purchase the wreck of *Lizzie May* as a bare shell. This would help offset the shortfall of the insurance payout. As a consequence, I became the proud owner of my *Lizzie May* all over again – even if she was an unrigged carcass, forlorn under a tarpaulin in the corner of the yard! At least she was not old and rotten which meant she could be easily fixed. For now though she would have to wait.

In order to speed things up I decided to overlap the start of William and Arne's new boat with the completion of *Agnes* by some five months, allowing us to bring the launch of the new vessel forward to the following spring of 2004. First we had to decide on what the replacement would be. *Lizzie May* was much loved and, at first, William and Arne wanted an exact replacement, even talking of taking such things as the tiller, doors, and deck furniture from the wreck in order to make *Lizzie May* live on in the new boat. It soon became apparent that making a copy was impossible. She couldn't be the same, times had changed, we had all moved on.

I had built *Lizzie May* during hard times, entirely with my bare hands, and I was not prepared to go through that again. I had since learned a lot about pilot cutter design, and was determined to put this hard gained experience into the next boat. Finally with many new ideas in the melting pot, we could see that this new vessel was going to be quite different, and so would need a new name.

Whilst Arne was more sensitive to the idea of a rebirth of *Lizzie May*, William realised that this was an opportunity to change and improve things as much as he could, building on what worked and discarding what didn't. In the end we came up with a boat more suited to their needs: bigger, deeper, taller, with more internal volume to accommodate the gadgets that William so wanted!

This new vessel was to be called *Hesper*, after the Greek for the first star in the evening sky, the 'Western Star'. She was to be 44 feet on deck, two feet longer than *Lizzie May*. This may not seem much bigger but it does make a surprising

Facing page: *Assembling the centre line, the stern-post is up and the stem is being lifted into place.*
Below: Hesper's *lines. Note the cutaway forefoot, a special request of William's.*

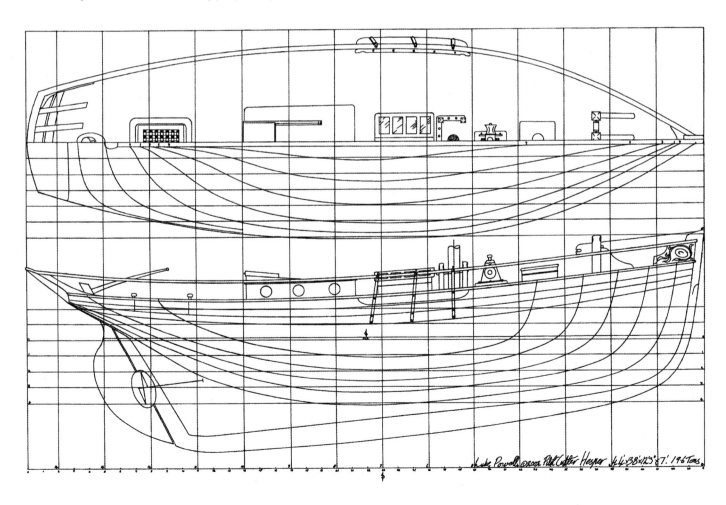

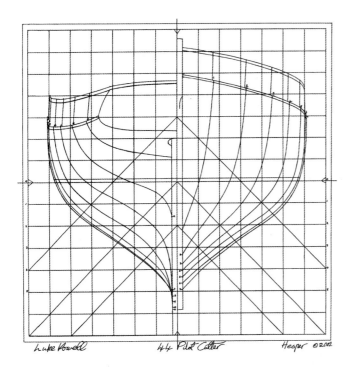

Luke Powell   44 Pilot Cutter   Hesper ©2002

on, everything was about meeting the stage payments. As far as my professional head was concerned, it was a relief once *Agnes* was launched and away. I could now concentrate on *Hesper*.

For some time I had been accumulating a good stock of oak. This is a tough and robust wood and its use can add to the life of a boat by a good many years. I also felt it was right to build with indigenous woods as they are more sustainable than those coming from West Africa, where forests are being felled with no thought of replanting. Cutting down trees is perfectly fine if you replace them. This is the natural cycle of things. Timber that is cut down locks up carbon while the replacement young tree is capturing more. All this is good for the planet.

Deforestation is another story altogether. This is the process of clearing trees from the land so that it can be used for other purposes. If we do not buy the timber then the trees are no longer valued and replanted and the pressure to use the land for other crops will encourage the burning of the forests, thus

difference. When a boat is longer it is larger in every dimension. A simple analogy is blowing up a party balloon; to make it an inch longer one needs a lot more puff and increased volume. Preparing to start *Hesper* whilst building *Agnes* meant burning some midnight oil. Once she was on the lofting floor, with Andy's help, we set to and quickly things came together. The first stage of the build is straightforward, a process of chopping up great piles of wood and, like a giant jigsaw puzzle, assembling them. The more complex task of finishing *Agnes* I oversaw from a distance, leaving Jonny, Will, and the electrician to get on with their respective tasks.

Over the years William, Arne and I had become close friends. The building of a boat is intense for all concerned and we had been through a lot together. I sometimes feel like a midwife to the owners. This was our second baby together and, after the near death experience with *Lizzie May*, a strong bond had been formed.

Once we started on the planking, *Hesper* took shape. Despite the stress of working on two boats simultaneously it had paid off. We were on track for launching the following spring. Keeping tabs on both projects proved tricky, but the lads worked well and knew their tasks. I am sure they felt that they could get on quite happily without me. That said, it was my job to push the pace by keeping the pressure

Top left: Hesper's *body plan.* **Above:** Hesper's *stern from above showing the framework of the counter. Note the yoke that sits astride the stern-post, this takes the weight and stops any spreading.*

Facing page: Hesper *all framed up and basted with a mix of linseed and tar. She is now ready for planking.*

clearing the land for the grazing of cattle, the planting of maize and soya for food, or sugar cane for biofuels. The burning of the forests causes a massive discharge of carbon into the atmosphere and destroys any chance of regeneration. How can we halt all this madness, when those who are supposed to lead us and safeguard our future spend their time rearranging the deck chairs on the *Titanic*!

Half the reason I build boats, and I am sure the same reason people buy them, is that in the back of our minds when it all goes wrong we can escape, sail away to nirvana. Personally, my own needs are simple. All I want is to be left in peace in a secluded valley with a good woman and a boat to build.

Hesper in frame with her sheer strake on, as launch day approaches for her sister Agnes.

So I resolved to use oak for *Hesper's* topsides. The stock of oak had not been with me long, not enough to be certain that it would not shrink. I cut out and dressed the planks, but decided to leave out every alternate strake, with the idea of driving these in later. Instead, we carried on down the hull into the lower larch planking, continuing down to the bilge. Stopping there, we began again from the garboard strake, working upwards. This proved to be a wise practise, as by the time we finished planking the bottom, the top strakes had been drying for two months. We were now ready to drive these home and, once in place, *Hesper* proved to be tight as a drum.

The sense of achievement was considerable. We were all proud of what we were creating. Everyone knew their jobs. I just had to learn to step back and allow the guys some space, which was not usually in my nature! Jonny has an engineering mind and is good with metal, so I asked him to make all the iron fittings. Considerable trial and error was required to perfect designs that were both strong and authentic. The original boats would have had forged iron fittings, beautifully wrought with furnace and anvil. We were fabricating ours from welded steel, but it was still important that they looked the part. This meant a lot of beating and grinding of the welds to suggest hand-forged organically grown ironwork. Created by hand, every little detail had to be right. It would have been so easy with modern tools to end up with a boat that looked as if it had been created by a machine. It's all in the detail!

I aspire to the principles of perfect form and function held by William Morris in the Arts and Crafts movement. Morris's belief that you should have 'nothing in your home that you do not know to be useful or believe to be beautiful' can easily apply to boats. My role is to make sure that everything on board looks harmonious. Time spent getting things to look just right is never wasted. On any project it is important that one person with an artistic eye take control of continuity in style throughout the build.

Things had to be done in an authentic way and as close to the original as possible. If we were building good replicas then we should try to build the genuine article. I retained control of certain aspects of the build that were important to the structure. For example the framing up of the counter-stern, the checking the fairness of the hull, cutting the sheer, and fairing the line of the planking. The same was true of some of the detailed fittings, like the rudder-trunk, beam shelf, lodging knees, knight-heads and stanchions. All needed to look right. It was not that I was more skilled than the others, but in my mind's eye I knew exactly what was required. I alone had researched these vessels down to their every last detail, poring over the old photographs, paintings, and models. So it was easier to do it myself.

Once finished on the hull planking, Andy began fitting the deck beams. A fine craftsman, he could cut in the dovetails with his eyes shut. I may have had an eye for the boat but he had a feel for his tools and I was fortunate to have a man like this on the job. Sadly, Grant was no longer with us as he had decided to go back to New Zealand to become a 'Possum Ranger' in a game park. Will was still wielding a paintbrush, still a frantic youth. He spent a lot of time

Above: *Most of the planks are fitted, as we now work up from the bottom. Note that the second and forth strakes from the top are not in place, this is so they can season before fitting.* **Below:** *Drilling and fastening a plank while Andy spiels for the next one.*

Above: Deck beams and carlins are in place and the stanchions are being fitted on the port side. *Below: Andy is shooting off the bevel, preparing for the shutter plank.*

chasing after Andy, scraping off the hardened glue that had oozed from the joints and scarfs.

William and Arne frequently came down from London to inspect the progress, bringing with them a Fortnum and Mason picnic hamper and extremely smart friends from Chelsea to see us artisans at our toil. It was amusing to watch Will, a rebel of noble stock, and Andy a beatnik socialist, as they bristled, finding it difficult to stoop and tug their forelocks. Jonny, on the other hand, was oblivious to all this, being too preoccupied with his own class war with the management by leaving cryptic Trotskyist messages intended for me, chalked randomly about the boat, always where he had been working. He never quite understood how I knew who was writing them.

William enthusiastically enjoyed the process of having *Hesper* built. It was something he had missed with *Lizzie May* as she was nearly finished by the time they bought her. He proved a formidable researcher, and quick learner. Nothing escaped his attention, from light fittings to propellers. He taught himself all he could about the gaff rig and the wooden boat. As *Hesper* grew, he quizzed me on every aspect of the build, from why we drive a tree-nail into the heel of the stem and stern posts as stop-waters, to why the stanchions are dropped down through the cover-board rather than the cover-boards let in around them.

Everything has a cause and effect. It is imperative not just to know how to make a boat but also its function and behaviour when at sea. This allows one to make the right decisions during her build. The only down side to William's involvement was that he would phone me any time of the day or night, so that I often spent my Sunday evenings, with baby Esme on my knee, chewing through ideas that had been niggling him. Bless him for his insatiable enthusiasm. This was such a contrast to the experience of *Agnes* and Shel's detachment. It must be fabulous having a boat built knowing that a bunch of craftsmen are striving to create a thing of beauty just for you, that when they have finished you can take command and sail it away. How I should love to have this done for me!

As *Hesper* took shape the decision-making became more complex: which fastenings for the decks or types of wire for

Above: *Will is set the task of caulking her bottom.* **Below:** *We are now moving ahead fast. The hull is caulked and stopped. Jonny is fastening the stanchion, while Andy lays the deck.*

the rigging? Then there were the windlass, stern gear, rudder pintles, light fittings, steering gear. The questions were endless. Should she have an automatic pilot? If so how could we provide the electricity for it? Maybe a generator, but what sort, or perhaps solar panels? Not to mention what sort of heating system. Should she have a heated towel rail? How many radiators? What about a water maker? Black tanks…grey tanks…blue tanks… All this on Sunday nights with a baby on my knee! One thing was for sure, it was as steep a learning curve for me as it was for William.

All I have ever been interested in is the past and creating new old things. I have a talent for making things look instantly aged, even before they are finished, and would have made a good forger of antiques. This talent lends itself to the building of authentic historic replicas, boats from another age, even down to the wooden buckets, cast iron deck pumps and a coal range to cook on. So too with the blocks and tackles to handle the sails and an authentic hand-spike barrel windlass to raise the anchor – this is my true vocation, all has

Launch day and Hesper *blows out of the Helford like a cork out of a bottle, with a grinning William at the helm.*

to look like the real thing. The idea is that when you are out there, away from the land, with nothing in your field of vision to offend the eye, there is nothing to remind you of these modern times. Then and only then comes true happiness.

But life has its compromises and I realise that we live in the twenty-first century and some concessions are inevitable. An engine was fitted, as were electric lights. *Hesper's* hull was painted not tarred. With William I was being dragged kicking and screaming into the new century. I would have to learn about heated towel rails whether I liked it or not.

William was precise about the finish of every aspect of the boat. I realised that if I could learn from him it would stand me in good stead for the future. He raised the bar, taught me to understand the needs of the owner. If I had spent this much money on a new boat, then I would expect some creature comforts. I had to understand that things like hot running water and a refrigerator for the cold drinks should be a matter of course.

Even deck leaks, always part of life on a wooden boat, are now seen as undesirable – specially on one full of sophisticated expensive electronics. Owners are even insisting on dry bunks! In the past I had always caulked the decks with hot pitch in the old and accepted way, but this requires regular maintenance. When a leak appears a hot knife has to be applied. So as part of my re-education by William I had to make another concession to modern life – synthetic caulking compound! Unfortunately, after launching, the compound proved ineffective and started pulling away from the seams in long ribbons. It had not adhered to the wood properly, which meant several days pulling it out and starting again.

In a moment of weakness I gave in to an electric anchor windlass on the foredeck. The next battle was over sheet winches. This time I dug my heels in. In the end, after a long standoff, I agreed that we would strengthen the deck in the area where he wanted the sheet winches, but *Hesper* would be launched without them. We fitted her with the traditional

Hesper *below. The work is done and the wood shavings are swept away.*

Samson posts and this is how she stayed until after a few years William felt the dust had settled enough to safely hack off the posts, making way for these big bronze beasts.

In truth, it all went pretty well and I absorbed many new ideas from working with William. Each customer has an input which, after sifting through, leaves me with new ingredients that get incorporated into the mix and improve the end result. For this, I must thank William.

Hesper was launched in April 2004, a year after *Agnes*, proving that if all went well we could build a boat a year. So the team was disbanded. Will went off to walk the Hindu Kush. Launch day was a quiet affair, just immediate friends and the work force. Once in the water the sea trials were as they had been with *Agnes*. In windy conditions, *Hesper* came out of the Helford River like a cork out of a champagne bottle; immediately the sails were up she was away, sailing as if she

had been doing it forever. Straight into her stride, she was as impatient as William to wash the builder's dust from her decks. With William at the helm, grinning from ear to ear, she heeled to the wind and swept away across the bay. Within a week the handover was completed. William and Arne were happy and confident. Having already sailed *Lizzie May* they were old hands at this. So off she sailed east, around Dodman Point, to the start of her new life.

A party for *Hesper's* christening was held at her home port of Fowey, where she was moored alongside the quiet little quayside at William and Arne's house, Prime Cellars, an idyllic place for her baptism. It was where she belonged. Seeing her there was like seeing an old girlfriend in a new life. I was able to smile and wish her well. The party was a glorious affair in baking sun, with a hog roast and barrels of beer. As the tide lifted we piled on board to float downriver,

streaming bunting from every halyard. As the night drew on, we said our farewells and returned home. I felt a little sad at leaving the water.

How I longed to live my own life afloat again, on the water, but one day... one day my time would come.

Facing page: Hesper *at her new home of* *Prime Cellars in Fowey.*

Below: *Wth her jack yard topsail set, looking good as she heads past the mouth of the Helford River.*
Right: Hesper *alongside the quay at Prime Cellars.*

Lizzie May *amongst her peers at*
Fowey during a Pilot Regatta.

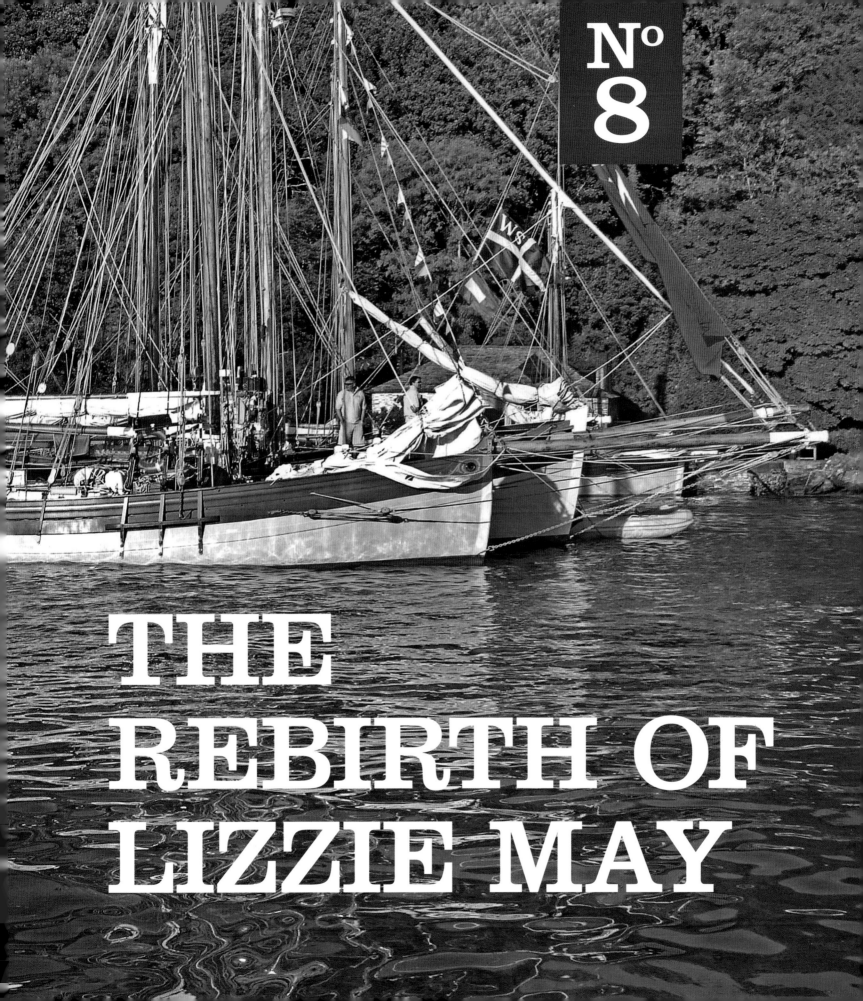

THE REBIRTH OF LIZZIE MAY

There is always a strange moment when a boat leaves, especially on returning to the yard, finding an empty patch of ground where once she stood. It is almost as if she never existed.

On returning to the yard after *Hesper's* launch I had to pinch myself in order to gather my thoughts for the task in hand. What next?

Whilst *Hesper* had been rigging out, the hulk of *Lizzie May* was dragged round to the building shed. Finally, after two years forlornly hidden in the corner of the yard, *Lizzie May* emerged. It was time to get the poor old girl back to life. This was something different, something personal. The next commission was not due to start until September 2004, giving me five months, so until then I had the chance to fix and sail one of my own boats. This was exciting, this was playing at life, just how I like it! The work force was now reduced to Jonny, Andy and myself.

The insurers had declared *Lizzie May* a total loss. To put her right, we had to cut out the broken wood and rebuild a wreck. *Lizzie May* had one thing in her favour. Being new, the wood in her was still supple and yielding. I think it was this that saved her. She flexed on impact, absorbing the shock that passed through her like a hammer on rubber. An old boat would have shattered like glass under the impact.

Left: *The wreckage, broken spars and hatches are stripped off* Lizzie May *to assess the damage.*

Facing page: Lizzie May *is back in the building shed for her repair, as* Hesper *in the background nears her launch day.*

Andy began chopping out all that had been smashed so that we could see the extent of the damage. I was amazed to find no broken frames or pulled fastenings apart from the two hull planks that had been punched out of the bottom by the compression posts amidships. The worst damage was to the deck structure, So off came the hatches, coamings and deck planking. Striped back, we were then able to see what we had and start the return journey, fitting the new deck-beams and carlins. Back went the deck, new coamings, coachroof, skylight and finally the bulwarks. Then we went downwards and re-planked the bottom. The last job was to make the new mast and spars and then rerig her. *Lizzie May* had come back to life; the phoenix had risen from the wreckage.

It is funny how things go, the misfortune and tragedy that befell *Lizzie* had in the end proved beneficial. The accident had given me a new commission to replace her, and additionally the chance to own one of my own cutters. That is if I was

prepared to plough a good amount of time and resources into her. They say 'its an ill wind that blows no good!'

My principal motive was the excitement of being a sailor again. We decided to get her ready for Brest 2004. *Lizzie May* had been a big part of my life; it would have been easier and cheaper to break her up. But the opportunity to race her at Brest against the other classics was a chance I could not let pass by.

Brest! That fabulous traditional boat festival held in Brittany every four years. I had not been there since the very first one on *Charmian* back in 1992. It's a fantastic event; full of beautiful boats from all over the world and is an experience that people like me live for. I was determined to go back, and this time *Lizzie May* was coming with me!

To get *Lizzie May* ready on time was touch and go as we only had a few months to rebuild her. It meant omitting any luxuries,

such as an engine and electrics. In fact this was a fine excuse as it was a pleasure to get back to basics.

I took off the propeller and filled the prop-aperture in the rudder and sternpost. The mechanical windlass on the foredeck was removed and replaced with a wooden barrel windlass, operated by capstan bars. After all the concessions on *Hesper* it was time to clamp down on free thinking. A barrel windlass was now to be compulsory on all Working Sail boats, whether owners liked it or not!

Lizzie May was my therapy for the compromises that had been forced on me in the past. She would have oil lamps to light the compass and running lights. Hand pumps for fresh water. A new clinker dinghy was built instead of an accursed rubber 'deflatable'. I was realigning my principles; reasserting that a boat can be simple and sail quite happily without all the techno clutter. The simpler a boat, the less to go wrong.

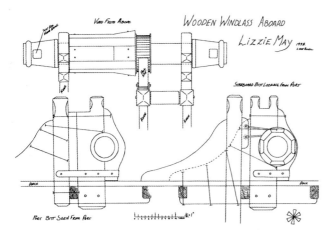

Drawing up the barrel windlass for Lizzie May's new life.

All too often the modern yachtsman will throw technology at his boat in order to compensate for his lack of seamanship. A good example of this is the 'bow-thruster'. No yacht under two hundred tons needs such a thing and, to me, it just shows that the owner is incapable of manoeuvring his boat and so should not be in command of her. In the same way his fear of the sea makes him fill the chart room with no end of gizmos. Can he not navigate? If not, then rather than just throwing money at the problem, go to school, put a little effort into it. Creating a comfort zone is no substitute for time spent learning the ropes.

Lizzie May was now a lean, stripped back, racing machine, the pure essence of a boat. She came together rapidly. What would have been a year's work for the unprepared was for us a piece of cake. It is amazing how much time you save if you don't dither, no talking endlessly about the best way to do things. Just get on! This is our trick and it makes an amazing difference in the time it takes to build a boat. We were fast at what we did because we knew what we were doing and wasted no time pontificating.

Lizzie May was in the water with only a week to go before Brest. The rig went back in, ropes spliced, sails bent on. Down went the tools; the shed was locked. Let's go sailing! On the early morning tide we shipped the crew aboard; Andy, my trusty shipwright, Big Nick, the ever faithful strong man and rope puller, Patrick our sailmaker and Sara with the kids, Esme, Oona, and Harry. The tide was not great and with the wind blowing upriver there was no chance of sailing from the quay. Luckily Clive Emerson was at hand and with a good heart he towed us out with the yard launch. We bounced from mudbank to mudbank, heaving and pulling and finally making it out into the tide just before it ebbed away. Setting sail as soon as we had a good fetch, the towrope eased and we cast off with a cheery goodbye. Clive smiled benevolently at our antics. We were away through the moorings, and with the wind in our hair, sailed out across the bay to Falmouth.

Lizzie May felt frisky and lithe without the propeller to slow her down; she was ready for an adventure. In Falmouth we met up with other boats preparing to sail south, in a similar position to ourselves, engineless, creatures of the wind. I spotted Spike with the smack *Ibis*, the luggers *Reliance* and *Guide Me*, and Ashley Butler with his bawley *Sally B*. With this good company we gathered in the anchorage awaiting a fair wind to cross the Channel.

That night a violent storm struck. It blew hard from the east, the harbour turned wild, and we started to drag. Despite putting out a kedge, we could do nothing to stop *Lizzie May* from driving helplessly across the harbour towards the docks and the splintered pilings at the far end. It is in these situations that boats without engines are easily lost. Luckily, as we swept past the pier, Jonny managed to get a line ashore. This took the strain just in time and thankfully held. We were soaked yet invigorated and by the time we had squared away it was dawn and the sun came up to an anchorage blown clear of boats.

Lizzie May beating out of Falmouth under Pendennis Point.

Above: *The French do it so well! Le Renard driving headlong off Brest.* Above right: *The wonderful Bisquine* Cancalaise *setting her main at Douarnenez.*

Above: *At Douarnenez 2004. Charlotte, Oona and Jess scull across the harbou*

Left: *The* Bessie Ellen *sails into St Mawes for the first Pilot Cutter Championships.*

Below: *The bows of* Mutin *and* Etoile, *both owned and sailed by the French Navy.* **Above right:** *The schooner* Fiddlers Green *at Douarnenez festival.*

The wonderful Bisquine Cancalaise *about to sail through the Tas de Pois off the Pointe de Penhir in Camaret, Brittany.*

Gradually the wind blew itself out, settling to a gentle breeze. It was time to extricate ourselves from where we had fetched up. We shook out some canvas to get clear of the land and headed south on a fair wind, chasing after *Sally B* and the rest of our little flotilla. It was good to be free of the land. In mid Channel and the middle of the night we lost the wind. Then the fog set in like a warm glowing blanket around us.

As day broke with the slightest of winds, we closed in on the French coast, passing a friend going the other way in his Vertue. Having lost the use of his engine he had decided to put back to

England thinking it imprudent to continue under sail alone. We glided on, with *Sally B* now in sight on the horizon but also making little progress. We sailed on into the next moonless night. Stars filled the sky as we passed through the Chenal du Four, ghosting along, just keeping steerage. With hardly a breath of wind the sea was like a mirror.

Esme, only four years of age, came on deck in the stillness. In the light from the compass it was beautiful to see her excitement at counting the flashing lighthouses all around the horizon. 'What are they daddy?'

Dawn arose and the breeze filled-in as we turned in towards Brest. By noon we were approaching the harbour on a broad reach, only to be met by boats of all sizes and shapes pouring out of the harbour mouth. Although weary, we turned about in mid-stride and went out to play with the others.

What a fantastic time it was in Brest. We raced and sparred by day, drank and made merry by night. *Lizzie May* proved herself well. I was amazed at what a difference it made, not only without the propeller, but having filled in the prop-aperture as well. She was like a different beast, she was special, she was mine. She could turn on a sixpence whilst tacking through the crowded festival harbour, however tight the manoeuvre. She could do all that was asked of her; luffing up in narrow gaps and working through fickle winds that backed around buildings, never losing steerage or getting caught in irons. It was a joy to sail her, and I defied anyone to catch us!

After the two weeks in Brest and then Douarnenez, we were exhausted. Wearily, we set sail heading north by west, seeking refuge in the open sea away from the drink and the bars. Never again would I touch another drop! Away we went, next stop the Scillies, our spiritual home and the next challenge – The Round the Island Race.

Arrival there from the south is always a pleasant landfall. There are no threatening off-lying rocks but the land is low and not seen until close to; that way it seems to suddenly jump up at you. With St Agnes bang in front and a clear entrance to the Cove, we sailed straight in. This peaceful place always feels like home from home, perhaps reminding me of my childhood in Greece. We dropped anchor in the clear blue water. Then before the sails were stowed Captain Yow Hicks pulled up alongside in his punt to welcome us. It was good to hook up with the locals again, catch up on the gossip. A new baby is always the biggest news on an island of so few people.

On the first weekend in August there is a race around St Mary's to St Agnes. We were ready, out early, tacking back and forth, charting the narrows on the north side of St Mary's. With the tide ebbing I was not sure whether it would be passable by the time we got there, but I considered it worth a try. So, bang and the race was away. We got a good start driving to windward with the best of them. On one side was Keith Buchanan in his pretty little *Bee* and the gentleman buccaneer Diccon Rogers in the ancient *Kathlee*. On the other was good old Alf Hicks in his crabber the *Petit Fox*. We were all going well on a good breeze, cutting to windward and heading for the narrows of Crow Bar.

I turned to the St Agnes men on board, our local pilots, asking where the rocks lay, to which the reply was 'Wrong side of the Islands, don't know these parts.' Then crunch, we hit. *Lizzie May* jumped a foot or more out of the water on to a rock and lay over to leeward. At this the competing fleet tacked away as one, off through the narrows. Alf shouted back 'You're our depth-sounder, when you hit, we tack!' Being of shallower draught they just watched and waited, but we were not finished.

Kindly, one of the tripper boats came to our rescue with long warps, valiantly tugging at us. Heeling over with the sails still drawing, we bounced sideways and shot off at full tilt, sails pulling. We were away again, madly in the other direction, the tow rope skipping across the water as we went, managing only to cast off just before it pulled the stern out of the tripper boat.

Could we get over Crow Bar this time? No, the tide was ebbing fast now, the sandbar got us. We needed another tow off. Needless to say we were last home, rounding up into the anchorage to great applause from the Turks Head pub on St Agnes. Cornish wit is dry at its finest and best served with a good pint of 'Doom Bar', of which we needed a few!

Early morning in St Mawes, with three fine boats.
Lizzie May *and* Agnes *together, with* Eve *behind.*

Time had run out for the crew, so they shipped out early on the Penzance ferry, leaving me with only Big Nick and Captain Yow Hicks to get home from the Scillies. We set off in a pleasant southerly, intending to sail through the night to Falmouth. As the evening drew on, the wind stiffened and headed us from the east, making the thirty miles needed to gain shelter under the lee of the Lizard an impossibility. Instead I chose to cut in behind Lands End for the shelter of Sennen Cove.

As we closed in on the land the wind strengthened to a good Force Eight. It was gone midnight when we came under the lee of the land. Getting out of the lumpy seas that were driving down Channel, it was a relief to be in sheltered water. The night was pitch black, but we carried on, safely guided by the new toy we had on board. Big Nick had bought along a GPS, something I had not sailed with before, and now found most comforting, knowing our position as we came into this dark, black bay. The wind was ferociously scudding offshore. Big Nick watched the newly fitted echo sounder, waiting for five fathoms, then we would round up, drop sail and get the hook down. I was not worried about coming close into shore as we were in sheltered waters, at the bottom of the tide, with a sandy beach. If need be we could come right up to the beach, then drop back on the wind.

The echo sounder seemed to be stuck on six fathoms. Then in the dark I saw the phosphorescence of the beach. Quickly rounding up, I hailed Nick to get the headsails down, as we were about to drop anchor. Then without warning, out of the darkness behind us, and to my horror, I saw a wall of water coming at us, a tsunami some twelve feet high. With no time to turn the boat, I grasped the tiller. The wave hit – whoosh – right over the top of us. Everything was a blur. I was washed forward, breaking surface hanging to the shrouds.

'Quick Nick!' I shouted. 'Get those bloody head sails up!'

Somehow we were inside the surf and now with only the mainsail set, could not bear away into deep water. I rushed back to pull the tiller but to no avail. The next wave hit us again, right over. The jib was now under the bows and full of water, Nick was up to his waist heaving on the halyard. He shouted at the sail, the sea and me for giving him impossible tasks. The waves had swept straight down the companionway, and the skylight had been ripped open with all the ropes washed down it.

At a glance I could see the water over the sole boards, and Yow, who had been swept down the hatch, struggling to climb out

again. With the third wave there was a heavy thump as we hit the beach. She came down, crash, onto her beam-ends, rolling out with the undertow. The next wave hit full-square with the deck heeling towards it, us clinging to the rigging. Over went Lizzie May, up and over towards the beach, the mast down parallel to the sand, then a sickening crash, back up again. She was now helpless in the surf.

Quick . . . Mayday . . . but there was no VHF radio. Big Nick, up to his chest in water, pulled out a dripping mobile phone from his pocket. I rushed below to get mine from the chart table. As I made a garbled message to the coastguard, my voice shaking with adrenalin, maroons went up into the night sky above the lifeboat station at Sennen village.

The coxswain, walking his dog last thing, had seen us in the bay and knew we would soon be in trouble. All we could do now was to hang on for dear life. I stood by the mast and apologised to Lizzie May for losing her. Soon she would begin to break up. I could see myself at dawn, combing the beach for my belongings amongst the splintered remains, trying to keep away the souvenir hunters.

The lifeboat launched, we could see her lights coming across the bay. They stood off about a mile, outside the surf. What could they do? How could they save us? I could not abandon Lizzie May and leave her to die. Flares went up from the lifeboat, silhouetting us against the black cliffs.

Suddenly, through the waves, came a rib at full tilt, shooting the surf, up the beach. Out jumped the crew in dry suits. Wading across, one of the crew threw me a thin line and we pulled him aboard. I set to getting in all the line, miles and miles of it. Eventually, I could feel the weight of a large rope coming towards me. Once it was finally aboard, I passed it through the lee hawse-pipe, tying it around the mast. Our new friend, Jack, reassuringly said, 'Ok, now you're in good hands.' Immediately Big Nick shouted 'Hang on!' and grabbed him by the jacket as we disappeared under yet another wave. Jack came up coughing and spluttering. Between waves we struggled to get the hatches closed and the mainsail down and stowed, the jibs and ropes back aboard: pausing to hang on each time Lizzie May went under.

We now had radio contact with the coxswain through Jack, who turned out to be his son. 'Hang on boys,' came the soft Cornish accent over the radio. 'Be patient, we'll wait for the making tide, before trying to pull the stem out of her.'

Above: *The Cornish trading ketch Bessie Ellen seen here at Charlestown, back from Denmark. After sixty years away, she has only recently docked and has yet to be rerigged.*

Below: *The other iconic Cornish vessel is the Irene, seen here at Fowey after her rebuild. She had been burnt to the water in the Caribbean, and was only saved thanks to the determination of her owner.*

So they stood off, just keeping the strain on the towrope. Each wave threw *Lizzie May* up the beach. Every time we thought the head was coming around, it would be knocked back by yet another wave. But slowly, as the tide rose, there were signs of her stern jogging up the beach and the bow staying off.

I could not believe the spirit of this lifeboat crew in the cold and wet and middle of the night. The guys from the rib, and now a shore party were out in the surf waiting to catch us if we were swept off the boat. The coxswain and his crew were beyond the surf, working to pull us round and save us. Jack was helping Big Nick and me. I felt truly humbled at the goodness of man... a tear in my eye, I could have hugged them all.

Bit by bit the towrope drew *Lizzie May's* bow into the waves. They were going to save my boat! The coxswain radioed to check the bilges. He was not going to pull us off only to see *Lizzie May* sink in deep water. The initial shock of seeing the boat half full of water was alleviated when, on going below and pulling up the sole boards, the water rushed down to an empty bilge. The water had been trapped on top, and with the saloon lockers full, the impression was that things were a lot worse than they really were. I switched on the bilge pump and drained what I could, keeping a vigilant eye on the level. 'Please don't sink dear girl,' I whispered urgently. We had to get her off the beach and I feared that if she began to leak the coxswain would abort the attempt, leaving *Lizzie May* to break up on the rising tide. However, he persisted, and slowly but surely *Lizzie May* came head to the sea.

Now, the waves rolled down each side, no longer washing across her and driving her up the beach. On the top of each crest she picked up for a moment and jumped forward before smacking down again. Thump! The whole boat shook from mast cap to keel. Then again, a little further, only to bang down again on the hard sand. Our teeth rattled. As the water deepened she banged down all the harder and I thought I would lose my fillings. Gritting my teeth, I waited as she came down again. Only this time she did not strike. Suddenly she felt as if she was floating on an eiderdown of smooth gossamer. She was free, and pitched smoothly like a bird on the wing as she sprang out into deep water. I could not believe it. They had saved us.

The lifeboat towed us out through the surf and then stopped and slowly hand over hand pulled *Lizzie May* up to them. As we came out of the darkness the coxswain hailed, 'Blimy! If I had known how big she was I would never have tried.' We came alongside in the dark to be greeted by the crew.

There in front of me was a beautiful woman with long flaming red hair like a pre-Raphaelite painting. She too had volunteered to save our lives. I was in love – or in heaven! What good fine people, yet they just shrugged their shoulders, 'It's nothing, just what we do.' Unsung heroes every one of them.

Left: *Esme helming* Lizzie *out of Falmouth harbour as I sort out the mainsail.*

Below: *Setting the mainsails and getting ready for the first race at St Mawes 2006.*

Light winds as Agnes *chases after* Lizzie May *at the first Pilot Cutter Championships.*

As the sun came up we lay to a mooring and began sorting out the mess aboard, pulling soaked bedding up on deck. To my amazement *Lizzie May* was not taking a drop. The bilge was still dry. As we rested in the morning sun, whoosh … bang … up went the maroons again and down its slipway went the lifeboat again. A yacht punching the tide around Lands End and making no progress decided to call out the lifeboat for a tow. A coxswain and his crew must have the patience of saints to let their time be wasted so unnecessarily. Needless to say, I will always be gratefull to those good people of Sennen. We sailed away on a calm misty sea, happy to be alive.

A week later it was all back to normal and we were racing in the Falmouth Classics. A stiff wind met us and we drove *Lizzie May* hard. She was none the worse for all that had happened and loved it. Although she did have another near miss with destiny, this time in the shape of Martin Heard and his pilot cutter, the 46 feet *Marie Claude*. We were beating to windward in a strong onshore wind, tack for tack towards the outer mark. Soon we were converging on opposite tacks at a combined speed of

sixteen knots. Martin told his helm to hold his course. They stood on. We stood on, just ahead and on the starboard tack. I was not giving way, and Martin never does! 'He's going to hit, stem on, amidships. He'll cut us in two!' But still their helm did not falter. I looked on stunned as their bowsprit end swept past our shrouds, only feet away and caught the leech of the main before sliding by. Thirty tons of cutter charged past our stern. I could have slapped Martin on his bald head as they thundered by. 'Have you next time!' he cried with a grin and was gone.

It had been a good summer's sailing and now we were back home with *Lizzie May* at her mooring. Some have said that she must be an unlucky boat to have suffered so much. I on the other hand consider her lucky. Considering all her adventures, all that has happened to her, she has survived every trial put in her way. From being squashed by a crane, to riding out storms and groundings. Where a lesser boat would have perished she shook it off and went on for more. She is a boat with a fighting spirit, and will go on, long and far, outliving them all. Good old *Lizzie May*. God bless her.

Launch day and Ezra is lowered into a dry river, but soon she will float as the tide makes. On the quay in the centre is Jim Baker, the latest member to our team.

EZRA

After the summer, away from routine, it is always good to be back in the yard with renewed energy. Ravenously getting one's teeth into the next project.

As our futures seemed more settled and new opportunities opened up, Sara decided to involve herself in the Falmouth Marine School. It was a place I had no time for, but she convincingly argued that if you want to change something it must be done from within. One of the first students on the boatbuilding course she helped set up happened to be Sam Brooke, a Manxman of small stature, but an ex-marine, as tough as nails, and a keen mountaineer whose hero was the Arctic explorer and yachtsman Bill Tillman. Sam's partner Ingrid, an equally resilient Shetland lass, is a lovely lady of few words blessed with a wonderful inner calm.

They had come down south to take a year away from the Scottish weather and a charter business in the Highlands. Having seen *Eve* sail in the harbour, Sam felt that this is what they needed, a real boat! But if they were to own one, he wanted to know how to look after it and so had joined the boatbuilding course. A wooden gaff cutter would be perfect for their charter work in the Western Isles.

One day we called in at their house for drinks and after several glasses of single malt and conversations about Bill Tillman an announcement was made – they intended to commission a new 44 ft cutter. Like Tillman, Sam wanted a boat capable of sailing into the Arctic north and other remote

Above: *Cutting the garboard rebate into the keel before it is set up. Here Andy finishes it off with a rebate plain.*
Facing page: *Shaping Ezra's keel, Andy cuts the mortise at one end while I do the same at the other.*

parts of the world. So *Ezra* was conceived. Named after an early Scillonian pilot cutter, she was to be registered at Lerwick in the Shetlands, a cold and windswept place far from Gweek Quay. So the night went on and we drank to her future health.

The next morning, still a little groggy from the previous night's libation, I began designing a cutter sufficiently stout and robust enough for the hard life *Ezra* was destined to lead. My starting point for the hull shape was *Agnes*, whose lute stern, square forefoot and V-shaped sections were ideal. With *Agnes* I had come close to creating a truly authentic Scillonian pilot cutter. She had the internal volume essential for charter work, with many bunks and much stowage space, yet she was seaworthy beyond measure.

So in the summer of 2004 lorries started to arrive with the timber from John Barchard of Hull. Andy Cornish, Jonny Albrecht and I were the building team, so we set to and rolled up our sleeves. Beginning by cutting out the keel, stem and sternpost, deadwood and frames, we carefully selected the right piece of timber for each job. This fundamental concern in choosing each piece for its specific task is the test of a good boat.

Above: *At Gunnislake Woods in Cornwall with forester Mark Snelgrove, selecting trees for the masts.*

Left & facing page: *The building plans for* Ezra.
Bottom right: *Oak boards in stick drying nicely, ready for use.*

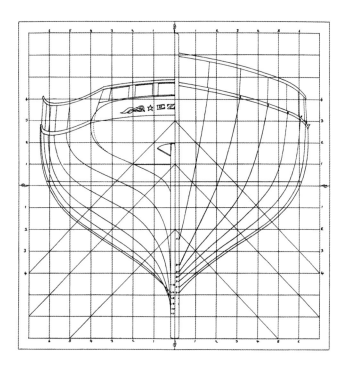

A readily available key timber in modern boatbuilding is larch. It is widely used for building Scottish fishing boats, where it works well in northern climes, as the cold kills off fungal spores, and the seawater effectively pickles it. In boats that put to sea daily, drenching themselves in seawater, larch is durable and hard-wearing. Also it is quick to season and easy to use. Three months of good summer drying and away you go. It is a lightweight wood, half that of oak. It steams well and is pliable, making it easy to bend into the curve of a boat's hull. Yet larch has it flaws. In recent years I have seen a surprising number of boats with new larch planking going rotten. This has been shrugged off for one reason or another, but the evidence does seem to suggest a worrying trend of premature decay.

Why is this happening? It is well known that larch suffers in fresh water: idle boats rot in the rain! But this is not the

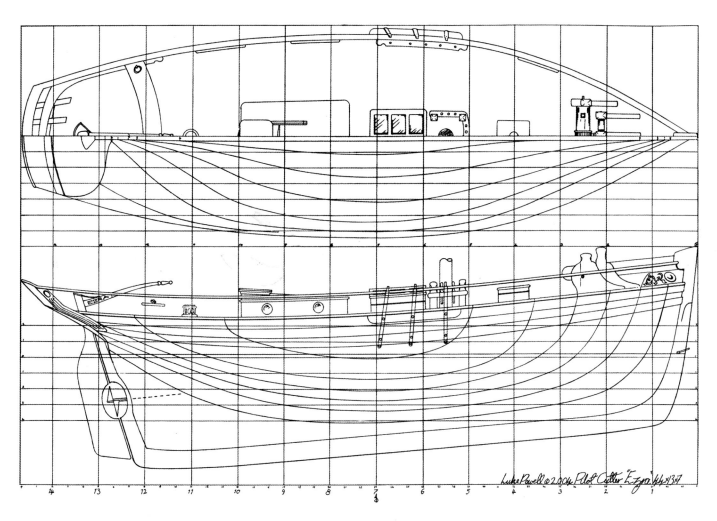

Luke Powell © 2004 Pilot Cutter "Ezra" 44'x13'7"

problem, there are other issues. One is that non-durable Japanese Larch (*Larix kaempferi*) is being mistaken for durable European larch (*Larix decidua*). The two timbers are difficult to distinguish, so the provenance of the wood you use is crucial. But more ominous is the fact that larch, like some tropical hardwoods, is prone to contamination from dry-rot spores, which infect the tree whilst it is still standing. The spores thrive in the leaf-mould of the forest floor and enter the root system. One must be wary in choosing the timber for a boat, as dry-rot spores can easily be carried into all that you build.

With larch there is another hazard called 'butt rot', the process by which a tree dies of old age. Contaminants are drawn up through the root system, thus starting the process of decay by making the tree rot from within; this is the natural cycle of life. The only reason it has become a matter of concern for boatbuilders is largely due to the demise of the wooden

145

Above: *Planning and assembling frames on the lofting floor.* **Below:** *Drilling out and then chiselling the mortises for Ezra's stem and sternposts.*

Above: *Assembling the deadwood structure, Andy is driving in one of the copper clenches.* **Below:** *Once all is fastened the centreline is then raised.*

148

fishing boats industry itself. In the industry's heyday, the British fishing fleet numbered in thousands. To build this fleet great stands of larch forest were planted specifically for boatbuilding, which in turn were felled at a constant rate. As the fleet reduced, the demand for timber dropped. The surviving trees have been left standing too long, so that when finally felled they are too old and 'butt rot' has already taken hold. Once felled, the timber darkened by rot is cut away up to where it looks clean. But infection will have spread through the whole tree, even though it is not yet apparent to the casual eye. This timber is then sent off to the sawmills and before you know it is being used in boats. I have learned over time to tell the signs of wood that comes from a sick tree, but they are subtle and larch should be treated with the utmost caution. If possible, inspect the stump of the tree as it is felled to make sure it is healthy. My advice is try not to use larch at all in the construction of the hull, and if you do then never above the waterline.

So far we had always planked the boats cold, without steaming the wood. For *Eve* I had a steam chest set up, but I was too impatient to waste time firing it up, preferring to get by with brute force and ignorance. Once employing others I was even more loathe to setting up a steam box. The thought of the workforce roasting chestnuts and warming their hands around the fire when they could be grafting was too much! However, was I being paranoid and misguided? Should I do something about steaming?

While we were building *Agnes* another interesting project had been taking place at Brightlingsea in Essex on the East Coast. Brian Kennel and a team were rebuilding a large smack called *Pioneer* that they had dug out of the mud. Once, whilst looking at their progress, I noticed their method for steaming – which they called 'boil in the bag'. Usually only a short part of the plank needs extreme bending, often in the tuck under the counter. The plank is clamped in place with the end that needed bending flying free and a long plastic bag, like a sausage skin, is slipped over the end of the plank then taped around to seal it. For the boiler they used an old beer barrel full of water which was placed over a wood fire, and a hose was then inserted into the plastic bag. Apparently this system worked fantastically well. So when the opportunity arose in this latest build I decided to have a go myself.

Facing page: *A watercolour by Anna Cattermole showing the 'patent' steaming set-up made of a converted beer keg and oil drum.*

The results were wonderful, changing my life. We stoked the fire with the endless piles of off-cuts. The beer barrel bubbled away and I made a canvas sock that inflated beautifully with the steam. Seemingly about to explode, it exhaled steam – sounding rather like a flatulent horse. Mixing the smoke from the fire with the steam we soon had the whole boat enveloped in smog. The beauty of this method is that the plank is already clamped to the hull. So once cooked, the bag is slipped off and the plank pulled home. No running across the yard with heavy scalding hot timber. Also, you only steam the bit you need to bend rather than having the whole board being in the steam chest. Another bonus was having no steam-chest to clutter up our limited yard space. But best of all it saved hours of time.

A cold plank took two people and a bunch of time to force in, whereas this way the plank was steaming while we worked elsewhere on the boat. When it was ready only one man had to pop back and with no effort clamp it into place. Of course this is where oak comes into its own, as a planking material there is no better wood for steaming. An hour of steam for each inch of thickness and it bends like rubber.

I remember as a lad being impressed when witnessing an old time shipwright, helped by the crew of the spritsail barge he was working on. They came to the bow with an oak board 3½ inches thick by 14 inches wide. After clamping it on, and with just their weight alone, they pushed it through 70 degrees around the bow. I was amazed that such a thick piece of oak could bend like a piece of lettuce. Another trick they had was to nail a thin piece of pine over the section of planking where the boat's name had been carved to prevent the short grain created by the carving from busting out. As the plank bent, the pine on the outside of the curve had to stretch further and was thereby held tightly against the carving and so stopped any rogue grain from breaking free. I liked this little touch; it showed a command of a situation and knowledge of their profession that is now a rare thing.

Ezra was built under the sharp scrutiny of Sam, our canny Manxman, but he did not need to worry. Boats built by Working Sail are my pride and joy and are intended to be my epitaph. From the apparent mayhem in the yard arises a phoenix of beauty. All effort is devoted entirely to the boat and not the business around it. This can be a bit disconcerting for potential customers, who are sometimes not reassured by what they see when visiting the yard. When we are building a boat there is a lot to look at, but when the boat has sailed away there is nothing left except a shamble of haphazard

Planking is coming along nicely. Once the hull is complete we turn to the top structure: Here Andy fits stanchions while I measure for the rudder trunk.

The deck is now on and being plugged before paying the seams. Then the hatches are fitted and the windlass is built and installed.

At last we have a boat. Ezra *looking proud and trim down below and on deck.*

debris, a residue awaiting our next creation. My reply to any critic of our method is to take a look at the boat, not where she is built.

With *Ezra's* hull now almost complete, she needed to be caulked. It is a job that, although I have done it many times myself, is good for any newcomer to the team, giving him something to get his teeth into and prove his worth. Two star pupils from Falmouth Marine School were given the chance to work with us, but we had only one place on offer. Both were keen. The younger, James Baker (Jim Bob) had the advantage in having more experience on boats. He had sailing parents and an eccentric grandfather, Bob Baker, who had been in the first wave of American wooden boat saviours back in the

but I tried not to let it worry Sam or affect the build of *Ezra*. Each day I came to work numb but determined not to lose control. I am sure that Sam and Ingrid must have worried that the storms I was weathering would take a toll on their boat, but they bore it well and held faith.

Luckily, the lads at work carried me through, but the business took a big financial hit. Years of hard earned money went into the divorce settlement and this meant that *Lizzie May* would have to go as well. This was the second time that I had lost a boat through divorce. Would I ever own another? How many times does one get knocked down in life and, more to the point, how many times can one pick one's self up again?

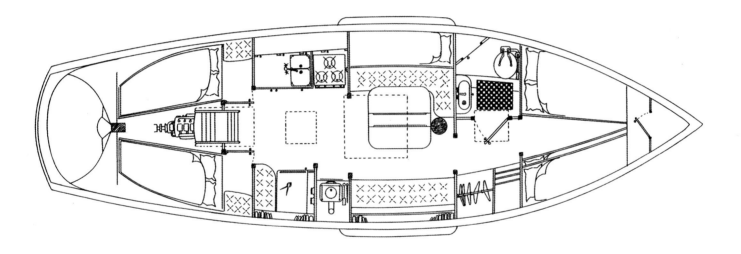

1960s. Ira, the other lad, had no experience of boats but was handy with a piece of wood. I set them both to the task of first rolling the oakum then caulking the hull – each to a side, thus a chance for healthy rivalry. Away they went and soon it became apparent that Jim Bob was possessed by a demon, driving full tilt along the seams, soon reaching the other end and back again, working down the hull at an eye-watering pace. I pitied Ira, who in any other circumstance would have shone brightly. But this was different, we had a man possessed by the wish to build boats. Needless to say Jim Bob won the day and became a good addition to the team.

Back home things were not so good, my marriage to Sara was slowly unravelling. The strain left me emotionally drained,

No sooner was *Lizzie May* on the market than several customers were eager to buy her. Simon Bell, a dashing, debonair writer from London, was the first to put the money down, buying her only twenty-four hours after she came on the market. This was a lot quicker than the first time she had been for sale, back in those dark years at Exeter.

Sara had been running the administrative side of Working Sail and so in the wake of the separation I had this new burden to deal with. Having never used a computer before and being quite dyslexic, I was on overload – just coping with keeping my head above water, sorting out the admin and trying not to lose focus on the build.

Away to
Scotland,
a stout ship
and a bonny
crew, Sam,
Ingrid and
baby Morag.

I worked on *Ezra* by day and struggled with the computer by night. To rub salt into the wound our accountant fell out with the bookkeeper and jumped ship without so much as a goodbye. In disgust at his behaviour the bookkeeper decided to walk. This left the business in a total mess with me barely aware of what was happening. The Inland Revenue was chasing me for late payment of tax and in my ignorance I had settled the divorce forgetting that the taxman wanted his slice. Suddenly I was being taxed for money I did not have. Hounded on all sides, it felt that by the time they finished there would be little or nothing left of me. Worse, I even had to borrow from the bank to pay the tax demands.

In time, life started to get back onto a more even keel. After several failed attempts I found a good accountant and a new bookkeeper called Nicki Hawkins who valiantly helped to sort out the mess. The tax fines came less often and slowly I clawed back my life. The one thing I learned from all this, apart from how to drink gin whilst smoking and listening to Leonard Cohen, was that the key to success in a small business is a good bookkeeper, and Nicki is the best. She's a lovely intelligent conscientious woman who saved my business, and with that saved my life.

Staying in business can be tough. Keeping the cash flowing and pricing the boats is always tricky. Not wanting to alienate potential customers, I try and keep my prices as low as possible. These prices are then printed in the brochure and remain unchanged for up to a year. It could then be twelve months before a firm order for a boat. Once the commission has been taken it could easily be another six months before starting. By the time we arrive at the last and most expensive part of the build, the fit-out, where the majority of the money is spent, it might be three years from when we originally fixed the price. Three years of inflation soon swallows up any potential profit.

In spite of these dark clouds there was a silver lining, news that there might be an opportunity to bring *Agnes* back from the United States. This was fantastic for me in my present state, as it gave me a breather, taking me away from the yard and all the troubles for several months. So I gathered a crew together, flew across the Atlantic and sailed *Agnes* back home. It must have worried Sam to see us fly off into the sunset, not knowing if we would return, let alone ever catch up with the work that needed to be done on *Ezra*.

The full dramatic story of *Agnes's* return is told in the next chapter, but once safely home again, and after a weekend in the pub to recover, it was back to work on *Ezra*. The fitting of the ballast keel, engine and tanks, was soon done. It was then full steam ahead with the interior. We were now chasing the deadlines set by her launch date. Sam and Ingrid had returned to Ardfern in Scotland to get the business ready for the start of their first chartering season. Much to their surprise, Ingrid was pregnant and Sam was uncertain how they would cope with their new life, the business and baby. Ingrid is a calm lass and her feminine nature allayed his male anxieties. Their website was soon running and bookings came in fast. People following the build of *Ezra* on my website were keen to experience sailing the new boat.

Launch day was set a year in advance, as the tides on the Helford dictated when *Ezra* could get downriver. Miss the tide and she would be neaped for several months, leaving the charter parties frustrated on the quay. So everything hinged on getting the work finished on time. We worked hard and managed to catch up on the schedule. The rig went in, paint applied, and all those final little annoying details that you get at the end of any job were dealt with. It was April 2006. Spring was here and she was now ready to launch. Sam and Ingrid came down to Cornwall for the event. It was great to see their faces, like kids at Christmas. *Ezra* had turned out well and happily Sam was proud of what we were about to give him. I think he was relieved that we had got through my divorce safely and that soon he would be earning a return on all that had been spent.

The days following the launch when the new boat is handed over are always stressful for owners. We sailed *Ezra* out of the Helford and around Falmouth Bay. Sam quickly gained confidence in his ability to handle such a heavy boat, learning how to run her short-handed. When Sam and Ingrid commissioned *Ezra* they were just a couple. Now they were three, as a beautiful little baby girl, Morag, was born only a month before *Ezra's* launch. Ingrid proved herself to be a natural mother, calm, capable and loving, but it did mean that the burden of sailing the boat fell on Sam, who at forty was a father for the first time. They are a fine couple and will cope with all that life deals them. I made them promise that one day we would sail *Ezra* to Greenland and climb Tillman's mountain. We had been through a lot together, including my 'midlife crisis'. So with damp eyes we hugged our farewells and they set sail away north to the West Coast of Scotland where the wild winds blow.

Day after day of empty sea, grey sky and constant wind. The north Atlantic in late September, it's the morning watch and my son Dylan takes his turn at the helm.

THE RETURN OF AGNES

Some days we sailed in thick fog as the wind blew at gale force. **Agnes** charged forward, ploughing her way across an invisible fog-bound ocean, us unable to see beyond the next wave. Some days the wind in the rigging was so strong it beat us back and I feared something might break.

Whilst building *Ezra* I received news from Gill Johnson, an American friend of Shel's, that *Agnes* needed saving. Shel's original intention had been to start an adventure school in Norwalk, Connecticut, just north of Long Island on the eastern seaboard, taking kids out to sea, gaining life-building experience. It was a noble idea and Shel, a teacher and good with children, was the man for the job. Unfortunately, *Agnes's* arrival in the States coincided with the economic downturn, which in turn affected Shel's ability to get the sponsorship he needed for the project to work.

Poor *Agnes*. At times she seemed doomed. One day leaving harbour she went the wrong side of the channel markers, running aground on iron piles. As the tide fell these drove up through her bottom planking, sinking her. It took a diver to plug the holes before she could be refloated. Then heavy snow during the winter that followed left her covered in a white blanket. An electric heater was put aboard to dry her out, but the extension wire used was English and not meant for the higher ampage of the American system. It overheated and caught fire, setting the saloon seats ablaze. With no one aboard the fire soon took hold, spreading fast. Soon the matchboarding of the bulkheads, locker fronts and shelves were ablaze. The heat became intense, cracking the glass in the skylight. Luckily, being laminated, it held, confining the flames to inside the boat. Having consumed all the oxygen, the fire filled *Agnes* with thick acrid smoke. Due to her being covered with snow the fire was unable to draw fresh air in from outside and so suffocated itself. Incredibly it went out, but must have smouldered for days.

Some weeks later, Shel came down to the boat and noticed traces of soot in the snow. He raked it back from the companionway, opened the hatch, and found himself confronting an *Agnes* thick with soot and as black as coal. Ironically, it was a miracle that no one noticed the fire when it was alight. If the hatch had been opened in an attempt to put it out, the air rushing in would have exploded in a potentially catastrophic fireball. Amazingly, *Agnes* survived. The saloon needed rebuilding, but there was no damage to the hull except some charred deck planking and a few deck beams.

The combination of a sinking followed by the fire unsurprisingly left Shel disillusioned with the boat, so he turned to Gill for help. Gill's intention was to use *Agnes* for chartering in the Caribbean. This came to nothing, and finally *Agnes* was laid up in a small backwater near Annapolis on the Chesapeake. A year later, amidst the tangle of my divorce from Sara, Gill contacted

Facing page: *The tiller was lashed for days while crossing the Atlantic.*

Above: *At last the sun is out and times are good, rafted up at Douarnenez.*

me with news of *Agnes's* plight. Desperately short of money, but aware that this might be my last chance to own a boat of my own, Shel and I began negotiations that ended up with my buying *Agnes*.

In late August 2005, having taken a break from work on *Ezra* and allowing myself six weeks to sail *Agnes* back home to Falmouth, I gathered a crew together. There was Big Nick, the ever faithful rope puller, young Jim Bob our enthusiastic sailing carpenter, and my son Dylan, who, at fourteen was strong and in need of adventure. As we flew over the North Atlantic I pressed my face to the porthole and peered down at the vast empty sea, wondering at the size of the waves. It looked cold and uninviting; a little ship down there seemed lost in that immeasurable emptiness.

It was night when we landed at Washington. As we left the airplane the hot and humid air of Virginia engulfed us. Taking a cab out into the darkness, not quite sure where we were going, I brandished a piece of paper with the address of a small boatyard up some creek. Once out of the cab, we found ourselves in the quiet sticky night walking down a wooden dock through lines of white plastic angling boats. On their aft decks were what looked like dentists' chairs – great padded fighting chairs festooned with an array of rod holders, weird fetish chairs for the American male ego to pit himself against innocent fish.

Then there was *Agnes*, strangely out of place, with the only wooden mast and looking much bigger than I expected. She rested gently, alone in a sea of moonlit plastic, shunned and separate from their world. Was this boat really mine? Had I once built it? Opening up the companionway I went below like an excited child, she was cavernous, so much bigger than I remembered. Once back on deck we opened an ice chest full of cold beer and in the warmth of the night we toasted *Agnes* and the adventures to come.

Next morning I came on deck to the din of endless traffic on the freeway flyover that stood high above us. In the sharp sunlight *Agnes's* attractions quickly waned. Paint was peeling and the varnish bleached. There were scrapes, chafes and war wounds. Not a paintbrush had been near her since she had been launched. Above water everything was tinder dry from the baking hot sun, below her hull was thick with weed.

'Hey there guys!' It was Gill, a man most at ease in a darkened bar with a bourbon on the rocks in his hand. He grasped my hand warmly. 'Great to see you.' He was friendly and generous in the way only Americans can be, running me to and fro in his car and helping us gather food, drink, some charts and spare rope. In two days we were fuelled up and away down the Chesapeake. But even with the sails up and the engine running, *Agnes* was so badly fouled with weed that she

could hardly move. Our first priority was to get her slipped before putting to sea.

Norfolk, Virginia, at the mouth of Chesapeake Bay seemed a good place to get the boat ashore. This was the land of the famous Skip Jacks, the sailing oyster boats, but those we saw seemed to be crumbling to pieces in the crippling humid heat. How could any wooden boat survive this intense humidity? Thank heavens we were taking *Agnes* north before she too ended up like the Skip Jacks, disintegrating with dry rot in the corner of a boatyard, boats whose days were passed.

The weather was overbearing, thick and soft with humidity. We were in the middle of the hurricane season. Sitting in a bar, sipping beer to cool down, the overhead TV showed hurricane Katrina wreaking havoc away to the south of us in New Orleans. It was time to head north away from this oppressive heat before another hurricane tracked up the eastern seaboard.

Agnes was antifouled and back in the water. Although the parched deck and open topsides desperately needed recaulking, we would just have to make the best of it. Victualled up and with new rope in the rig, we were ready to go. Despite our fears, we happily had an easy passage up the coast with genial warm

Below: *Big Nick takes his watch with renewed vigour.* **Centre:** *White water over the lee rails was a common occurrence.*

beam winds. I now could see how the great American seven-masters, slab-sided schooners, had so successfully plied up and down the Eastern Seaboard, taking advantage of fair seasonal winds. Loaded high with deck cargos of lumber, they were well suited to these conditions.

An invisible coast lay beneath the horizon. We sailed on peacefully, only occasionally disturbed by the drone of engines as an angling boat charged out of the mist, its fighting chair and khaki-clad men at the ready. They were as quickly gone, leaving only a wake as they headed out for the distant fishing grounds to do battle.

Arriving in Martha's Vineyard, a small sandy low-lying island off Massachusetts, we entered a bay sheltering a simple little town built of wood that seemed to rise from the beach, with streets of sand. Away went the anchor and *Agnes* came round to the wind not far from a fabulous large schooner named *Alabama*. Behind us, also coming in to the bay to anchor was the even bigger *Shenandoah*, over 100 feet long, engineless and splendid, built and sailed by the redoubtable Bob Douglas. She looked fantastic, a black giant ghosting in under square topsails, with great wooden-stocked fisherman's anchors at the cat-heads,

ready to drop. I was humbled at such greatness. Why can't we in England build wooden ships like this? Why are we so limp wristed? We do nothing to add a new page to our fine seafaring history. As Napoleon said, we are a nation of shopkeepers – and I might add, a nation of self-appointed health and safety officers. Hopefully one day we will have a renewed sense of adventure, enough to build a new *Cutty Sark*, make men of ourselves and inspire our children by sailing under full canvas through the Western Approaches.

Splash went the great anchors of the *Shenandoah* and splash went our dinghy. Over the side we jumped, rowing ashore in search of a bar – only to discover it was a teetotal town of Quakers. How was Big Nick to quench his thirst? After a short chat with some locals he was away, striding off over the hills, six miles to a bar that brewed its own beer. Having taken a liking to us as drinking partners, Gill arrived on the ferry. Excited by our shambolic adventure he had decided to come along for the ride. It would be good to have an extra man aboard, at least for the watches, and he was also handy with a spanner.

Our next port of call was Lunenburg, Nova Scotia. It was misty when we rounded the bleak headland that guarded the

Below right: *We drive on ever further over empty seas. All is wet, our bunks and our clothes. Nothing will dry.*

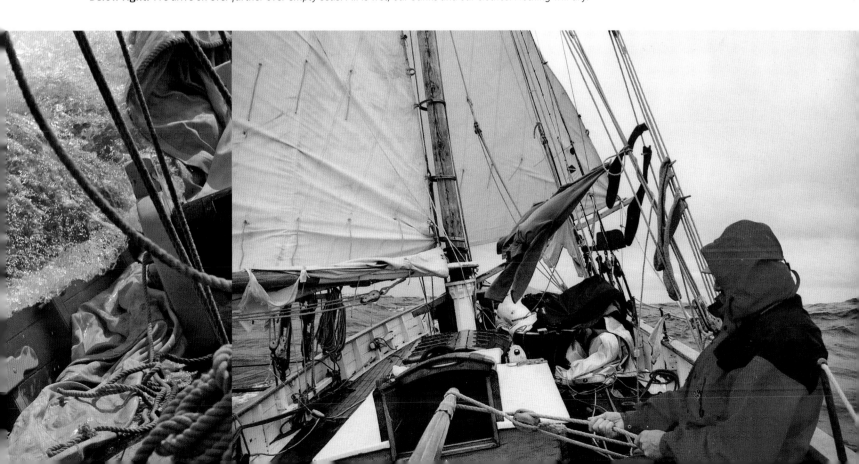

entrance. Impaled on a rock, like a dead man on a gibbet, a warning to all sailors, were the bleached bones of a large fishing boat. What had happened to this place? Only a few years before Lunenburg had been a bustling fishing port. Now its quay was deserted. Not a ship was left save a few derelicts at the fish-piers and a couple of tired old Grand Banks schooners tied up in tribute to the memory of the men who had served on them. The whole town was strangely quiet, as if life had moved on. The fishermen may have been out of work but at the one bar still open, 'The Not Inn', they sure drank their fill and for three crazy nights we were swept madly along with them.

It was now September, the peak of the hurricane season. Despite the forebodings of our new friends, we put down our glasses, reluctantly made our farewells and were away out into the Atlantic. Out past St John's and across the legendary Grand Banks into the deep where the winds blew and the storms thrashed. *Agnes* buried herself under a mountain of sea, which poured in through every seam. She would surely take up in time but our bunks were now soaked. We were wet through, our clothes as well as our bedding. We gave up shaving and slept in our oilskins. Only Jim maintained a semblance of normality, miraculously appearing on deck every morning cheerful and beaming with a fresh face and clean dry clothes. How did he do it? Someone must have packed him the mother of all bags!

We drove on, sailing over where the *Titanic* lay deep beneath us. The sea looked cold and inhospitable. The sky was dark and brooding, a menacing squall approached. Hoping to keep ahead of it, Gill put the engine on, when bang! The shaft coupling sheared and in the process bent the prop-shaft, throwing it back and jamming the propeller against the rudder.

There were shouts from above. 'I can't steer her!'

Quickly, from a deep sleep, I sprang from my bunk, diving into the engine room as Nick shouted down that we were about to broach. With all my might I dragged the shaft forward, freeing the rudder, but the bent shaft was beyond use. The engine was out of action and we had a long way to go. Out into an empty world where no ship or man lived. All was dark grey, sea and sky, night and day.

On we went, for days on end, reefed down and beating our way against damnable easterly gales. *Agnes* rode the Atlantic swell admirably. Where most boats would stall, she forged through without faltering, shouldering the seas apart. Some days we sailed in thick fog as the wind blew at gale force.

Agnes charged forward, ploughing her way across an invisible fog-bound ocean, us unable to see beyond the next wave. Some days the wind in the rigging was so strong it beat us back and I feared something might break. We then hove-to, giving us a respite from the ordeal. We caught up on much needed sleep, or just relaxed and played cards whilst *Agnes* lay calmly, staysail backed, helm lashed over, hull to the wind, riding the sea with the composure of a carthorse grazing after a day's toil.

When the weather eased a smidgen we went on, always to windward. But all the time we were slowly being pushed north, unable to make our true course. For two weeks I feared that we were not going to make it, but would instead be driven back to St John's or even further north to Greenland. Finally we managed to get south of the latest cyclone and miraculously, after nearly giving up hope, the wind veered to the south and then the next day to the west, moderating to a mild seven or eight. We were free! The reefs were shaken out, the sheets eased, and *Agnes* drove headlong, on course for home.

Back at Falmouth there was news of unusually violent *Atlantic* storms. No one had heard from us for three weeks. Our families and friends began to worry and fear the worst, thinking us lost at sea. The winds were still strong and life didn't get any easier but we were in good humour now and settled into the routine of life at sea. Dylan, a young teenager, slept and ate most of the time, but part of the deal was that he did school work in the mornings and took a stint at the helm in the afternoon. I enjoyed having him there – that good father and son thing – sharing the night watch and talking about life.

I drove *Agnes* hard, every rope and timber straining. We were making good progress, chewing off the miles in the daily log. The seas were still void of any ships but we were rarely alone. Pilot whales followed us by day and night. We saw turtles, dolphins, and the odd sperm whale. We nearly ran over one as it slept, only sparing it a rude awakening by swift action on the tiller. The great leviathan passed down our lee rail, scraping the boom end as it slid by. It was much bigger than *Agnes*, and god knows what would have happened if we had actually hit it stem on. Sometimes at night we could smell their breath on the wind, as t'was said of Moby Dick, 'When ye smell land, where no land be, then there he be'.

I whiled away my night watches pondering what to do once we were home. Sara wanted to sell *Agnes*. I on the other hand,

I just love it when the rain drives, the wind is foul and we have several days and nights to go!

having moved out of our large family home into a small terraced two up two down and having lost *Lizzie May*, found it difficult to come to terms with the situation. I could not afford to keep *Agnes* yet I loved this boat too much. Even out in the Atlantic, far from land, alone with her, a witness to how she courageously fought the seas, keeping us safe, I still could not see a solution. Then one night the stars came out for the first time in weeks and I had an epiphany. I would give the house to Sara. All I wanted was to keep *Agnes* and build boats. It was so simple. To live an ordinary life in a little terraced house or to live on a fantastic boat and have a life of adventure.

There was no choice. My heart sang. Why had it taken so long to work this out? I was happier than I had been in years. Life was suddenly fantastic. Out in mid ocean sailing *Agnes* with my son, all the troubles of land seemed petty and far away.

In time we closed towards the southern end of Ireland. The seas piled up as we crossed the continental shelf. For the first

time in weeks we saw a distant ship. A fishing boat passed, hull lost in the turmoil, but still no land. Then one morning on the horizon we spied far off something tall, thin and black. Gradually it gained in height and girth and then turned into a lighthouse – surely not, but yes it must be the Bishop Rock! The Isles of Scilly! We were home. With beaming smiles we watched the island of St Agnes slowly appear out of the sea. 'Land Ho!' Twenty-three days from Lunenburg and we came round the point into sheltered waters. Down went the hook into the calm waters of Porthconga, just off the 'Turks Head'. No sooner did we have the sails down than Big Nick leapt fully clothed into the sea to swim ashore, heading for the pub. After launching the dinghy, we were not far behind.

The next morning after the first full night's sleep for nearly a month we woke to the wind blowing hard into the bay. Without an engine we were trapped. It would have been ironic if after having travelled so far we were to be wrecked not twenty yards from where the original pilot cutter *Agnes* was stationed some

163

150 years earlier. But thank heavens for Captain Yow Hicks, who's always there when one needs him. Like a guardian angel of the Isles, he came round the corner to our rescue with his motor lugger, thankfully towing us far enough off to make sail and crawl clear of the menacing lee shore. Away we went, bound for Falmouth and home. That night the wind screamed. Ashore, doors were ripped from their hinges. Yet *Agnes*, with three reefs in, stood up to it without flinching. The only casualty that night was our dinghy, swept away, torn from its towrope. All we could do was watch on helplessly as it disappeared into the night.

Finally rounding the Lizard the wind moderated, dropping away to nothing. As we drifted into Falmouth, a blood red sun broke from the sea, pouring warmth into our souls. Traumatised with all that had come before we were unable to shake out the reefs and so becalmed, with the rig still snugged down, we shipped the sweeps and rowed her across the harbour to her mooring.

A great sense of achievement came over us. We were tired, thin, and bearded but had lived life to the full, though for a while the experience left me with a pit of darkness in my stomach, a trauma from having been out there in that vast bleak emptiness, where sky and sea were as one, a place for no man. There on the quay to welcome me was little Esme with Sara, five years old and shy at not having seen her father for so long. I rowed ashore to give her a big hug and she clung to my leg determined not to let go. We were home.

Agnes had to be mothballed, awaiting the finish of *Ezra*. The crew disbanded and Dylan with a manly hug went home to see his mother. So with Esme and some friends I sailed *Agnes* the final leg of the journey up the Helford River as far as possible until good old Clive came down with his launch to tow us up the last winding narrows to Gweek Quay. Esme took the helm as we tacked in the twisting river and the rest of us stood at the bow. She held the tiller above her head, whilst I directed her with small nods to push or pull. Valiantly she did her job with a proud beaming smile –the captain of our ship.

Once ashore and my batteries recharged it was straight back to work completing *Ezra*. It was now October, and she was due to be launched in April 2006. Spring came quickly. The launching followed, and free of *Ezra*, Andy and I could set to work on sorting out *Agnes* with our consciences clear.

The first task was to remove the bent prop-shaft. The biggest job was a major repaint, as every piece of wood

Calm water! Agnes *is home at last, safely at anchor in Bread & Cheese Cove, the Scillies.*

Above: *Esme takes the helm, with the total confidence of a child born to the sea.* **Right:** Agnes *is not just a boat, but also a time machine that carries one back to a finer age.*

needed scraping down and repainting. The mast, spars and rig required a complete overhaul. Because of the fire, a new saloon had to be built. She also needed two new runs of bottom planking to replace the short lengths that had been patched after the incident with the piles, a new forehatch to replace one stoved-in when in mid Atlantic, and repairs to the bulwarks where she had chewed up against piles in the Chesapeake.

Bearing in mind that *Agnes* had crossed the Atlantic twice, had sunk, been burnt and had no maintenance of any kind, she had done pretty well. Soon she was back to being as sharp as a pin, Bristol fashion and ready for sea again. By this time the best of the spring tides had passed, leaving the difficulty of getting *Agnes* with her nine feet draft downriver on feeble summer tides? I borrowed some pontoon flotation tubes, which I tied to her lower hull, hoping they would give sufficient buoyancy to reduce her draught and allow her to float down to the lower quay where the water deepened.

The morning tide came early. It was still pitch black when *Agnes* floated, high at the stern – so high that the prop was almost out of the water. Amazingly, we reached the lower quay

without incident. We tied all the ropes from the tubes to the quay and put *Agnes* into reverse. But the tubes stayed firmly in place under her. Their pressure against the hull stopped them from moving. There was no choice, the tide was falling and we would have to go downriver with *Agnes's* arse high in the air.

She was virtually impossible to steer, so we bounced from bank to bank. Rounding the first bend with the sun rising and the tide falling, we spied *Lizzie May*. She had departed earlier on the tide, but was now aground with Jonnie and a motley crew frantically sounding out the channel with oars. They were preparing to ballast her to starboard so she'd fall outboard onto the mud, rather than dangerously into the channel. Earlier they had laughed over our antics, but in the dark had missed a turn in the channel and were now stuck fast. Andy and I courteously enquired if they needed any assistance, offering them a line.

Taking the strain I put *Agnes* full astern to drag *Lizzie May* free, but she refused to budge. So letting the tow line run as I gave full throttle, then several turns on the bollards, *Agnes* snatched at the line, bringing her full weight to bear, using her inertia to pluck *Lizzie May* out. The tow-rope twanged like a harp string, *Agnes* lurched and *Lizzie May* leapt towards us and into the river, free from the mud.

Above: Agnes *is back at the Chain Locker Quay, Falmouth. Resting before the next adventure.*

Eventually we reached the lower river where we let go the hook. Moored nearby was Nick the diver on his old wooden trawler. He had come on deck in a dressing gown and stetson hat, his morning coffee in hand, to admire this early morning spectacle. I rowed over to him and asked if he would cut *Agnes* free. Casually he prepared his dive bottles, as if it was the most normal thing in the world, before breakfast, to untangle a pilot cutter from flotation tubes strapped to her keel. Nick descended, bubbles indicating his progress. Then there was the occasional twang of ropes as they were cut from under her. Then with an almighty upheaval of water the flotation tubes leapt from the sea like monsters of the deep and *Agnes* fell back into the hole. Nick was underneath and found himself

pushed down into the muddy riverbed. As the water settled, he surfaced – muddy but smiling.

It was the end of May. It was time for me to give up the house and move aboard *Agnes*. There was no point in starting another boat before the summer, so we shut up the workshop. Jonny was off to Douarnenez 2006, the amazing bi-annual boat festival in Brittany, on *Lizzie May* with her new owner, Simon Bell. Jim was getting his old boat ready, also to sail to Douarnenez, and Andy was off courting his new love, a gipsy circus girl. Me, I gave up my life ashore. Not since the days of *Charmian* had I lived afloat. Despite *Agnes's* size there was not enough space for the computer, all my books, half models, the plan chest and paintings.

After a chat with Clive, space was found in the building adjacent to Working Sail's shed. Once cleaned out this became my new office, and was soon to fill with all of the old stuff that accumulates when building boats.

This was to be my summer of realignment after the difficult years of heartache and financial troubles – a time to catch up. I went off to Mousehole's 'Sea, Salt and Sail' festival with *Agnes* and a boat full of friends. I was determined to surround myself with good people and enjoy the new found freedom of life afloat. Beautiful weather made it a joy to be alive, sitting on deck whiling away the evenings at anchor in some quiet bay. Next we were off to Douarnenez to race by day and swap yarns by night. What more could one wish

for? We drank, partied and sailed madly and by the end of it I felt purged of all that had come before.

On returning to Falmouth a good mooring was found for *Agnes* upriver at Penryn, where her neighbours at the quay were a raft of wooden fishing boats. With *Agnes* settled down in her mud berth for a winter spent as a houseboat it was time to stop enjoying life and get back to the yard and the latest cutter we were about to build. Time to work!

Below: *Inside my office at Gweek Quay. Jonny at the desk and all around him the paraphernalia of a business in boats, half models, dinghies, oil lamps, charts, ropes and the rest.*

Her first day out. Tallulah drives across Falmouth Bay at ten knots with little effort.

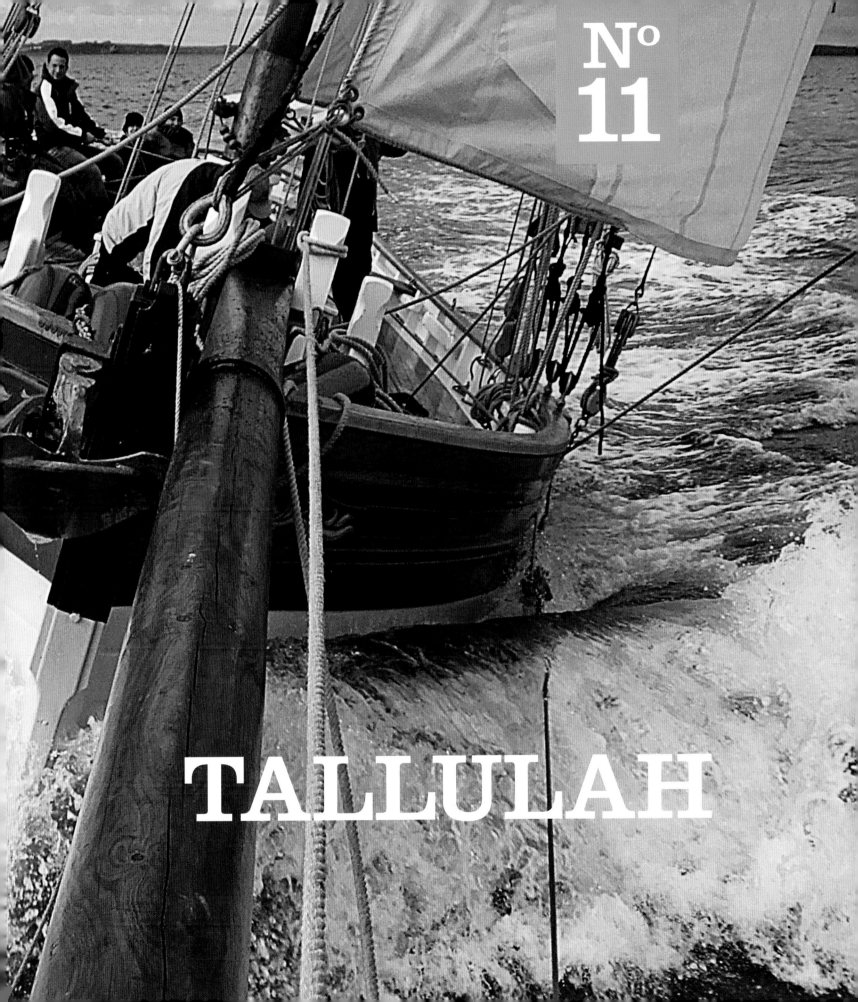

Nº 11

TALLULAH

By 2005 much had changed in my boatbuilding venture. I now felt established, the hard work had paid off, the boats already built were appreciated and enquiries for new ones were coming in thick and fast.

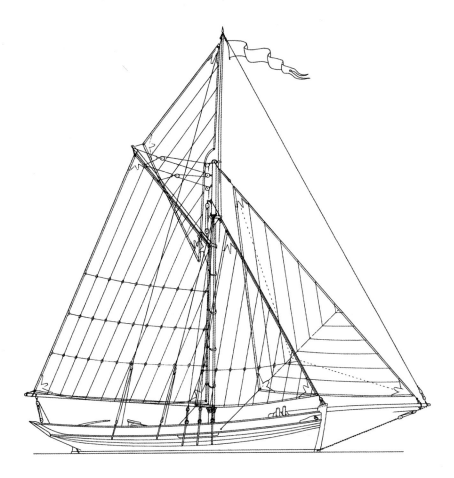

Reflecting on this success, I realised that it was due to the craftsmanship of my team and the boats being beautiful, not any marketing strategy or my business ability. Which brings me to ask, why is it that our emotions are triggered by beauty and yet why is it that so many people seem blind to its importance? Beauty in all its forms fills one with joy, and is what being alive is all about! If we accept that, surely the beauty of our environment equally matters? We seem to have forgotten the relationship between our emotional wellbeing and our surroundings. For example, why is it that so much modern architecture is downright ugly and inhuman? How is it that we now create urban environments that cause social discontent and a breakdown in the community?

My own opinion is that firstly we are obsessed by the need to be different purely for the sake of it, throwing out all that we have learnt, going against good practice, good proportion and visual aesthetics, in a headlong scramble to appear modern. Secondly, accountants rule over all decision-making, cajoling us into boiling everything down to its monetary worth.

Architecture, like much contemporary art and the endless rows of white plastic boats that fill our marinas, no longer has the confidence to believe in good taste. We the consumers are at fault. Frightened of being different, we lack the courage to stand up and shout 'No! Enough is enough!'

Every aspect of modern life is measured by the profit margin; best wages, best deal, cheapest food, fastest car, shiniest boat. What is wrong with this you may ask? Well, if things are judged only on their monetary worth, then all the abstract values of life that cannot be quantified in money terms are lost. Beauty, aesthetics, harmony, love and all that nourishes the soul, the poetry of life, are boiled away leaving us with a world designed by accountants with only two objectives – profit and to fleece us!

This is what is wrong with many modern yachts. The prevailing attitude today is that any aspect of the build that is seen as of superfluous expense is eliminated from the design. To improve the perceived value of the vessel it is designed from the inside out; beginning with the size of the fridge that can be fitted into the available space. Once this is decided,

Facing page: *Esme sits on the fashion-piece-yoke. Half built boats are a great climbing frame for children.*

a skin is drawn around the galley and called a boat. There is little thought as to how it will perform on the water or whether it will be seaworthy. Then, to add insult to injury, it is built out of a material that yields the highest profit margin for the least effort. What you end up with is bland objects with a uniform look, nothing more than the bare minimum. All too often the sale of this object is negotiated in a swanky showroom where the potential buyer is steered up the red carpet by an insincere salesman dressed in double-breasted-blazer. More time is spent down below testing the bunks and admiring the galley or electronics at the nav-station than on deck. Rarely does the customer cast a discerning eye over something that is about to

Andy takes a pause, content at having cut out a boat in kit form.

cost him a great deal of money, step back to see the lines, or take her out on the open water to evaluate her sailing qualities.

Many argue that such boats allow the 'ordinary' person to get afloat. Contentious as it may be, I believe that it's all too easy to acquire a boat without the ability to sail it ever being put to the test. Many boat owners lack any real knowledge of the sea and show no interest in it. To many, it is merely a place linking one marina to the next. So do they deserve to clutter

up somewhere that we hold so precious? There should be a task that all would-be owners perform before being allowed to purchase a boat – say a voyage as crew on a square-rigger, working aloft. Not only would that nurture a greater appreciation of the sea and an understanding of what a boat is meant for, it would also give a sense of personal achievement.

So having educated those that do take to the high seas, we could and should demand better of those who build our boats. The remedy is not always the construction materials, though this may help. So how do we build a beautiful boat? Firstly, there are the eternal rules of aesthetics as laid down by nature itself for all living things. A boat should be as natural in its element as a bird on the wing, as a fully-grown tree bending to the wind. A true boat is a living creature that has evolved through time to match its purpose and the waters in which it sails – in much the same way as Darwin explained evolution through the survival of the fittest. The boat that ignores these rules clashes with the environment and is at odds with nature itself. Like us, a pilot cutter lying at anchor is alive and like us she is mortal.

One's life becomes entwined in the very fabric of a boat, you live through it and it lives through you. Her balance of form, her line, the weight of all her constituent parts, the detail in the shaping of each piece of wood, all tell of our collective knowledge. As does the organic way in which she is conceived, from the half model to the lofting floor. From the forest come her bones and through the adding of piece upon piece she slowly comes to life. When at sea, she is in harmony with the elements and those on board will be nourished by their surroundings.

Amazingly, I had found a niche away from the harsh winds of the modern world, free to develop a business in an unconventional manner without commercial pressures. This situation suited my temperament, as it meant I did not have to work by the rules that govern so many of us. Hopefully, my success has encouraged others. Suddenly, within a year or so, there was an explosion of new would-be boatbuilders, most hailing from the Bristol area, building replica Bristol Channel pilot cutters. I could see the logic in hanging one's hat on a vessel with such a reputation as a fine sea boat, thus giving credibility to their labours. But I suppose my being so immersed in maritime history made me come at it from a different standpoint. How about reviving other types of boat that were extinct?

For me, this new competition was a little unnerving and made me aware that I was no longer alone. But maybe a new movement for wooden boats was gathering pace. Maybe our collective energy could create a critical mass able to repulse the tide of plastic! This I would like to see, nevertheless I was grateful for the ten years head start on my new competitors. The future seemed bright. Work was coming in and there seemed enough room for everyone.

My next customers, Victor Bradley and Ann Marie Colbert, were a gentle couple in their fifties. She was a teacher and he a partner in a firm of quantity surveyors involved in developing large architectural projects. Victor had a shrewd understanding of form and function and they looked closely at various boatbuilders. Having worked out what they wanted from a boat, they were able to make an informed choice. Or maybe I am kidding myself and the decision-making is more about the rapport between builder and customer. If so, then different types of people need different builders. My cavalier attitude is not for everyone. Victor and Ann Marie visited my yard a couple of times. We chatted pleasantly and I showed them over the vessel in build as well as *Agnes* at the quay.

After they had gone I never gave it another thought until one day in late December, whilst out taking Esme Christmas shopping, Victor rang and quite matter of factly announced that there was a cheque in the post for the deposit. It seems the less you push the more people want you. My plan was to start their boat the following September, giving time for *Ezra* to sail away, *Agnes* to refit, and me to move my home aboard and have a summer sailing.

First we had to discuss what sort of boat they needed. The answer was simple. One they could sail easily by themselves, not beholden to anyone and without a crew. I like Victor and Ann Marie. They are a quiet and kind, and I wanted to design them a boat that would be as light to handle as possible. She was to be named *Tallulah*, 44 feet long on deck yet only 37 feet on the water, giving her a long counter and slightly more rake to the stem. As *Tallulah* was just for the two of them she did not need a great internal volume. This meant I could pare away the hull to reduce the tonnage, which in turn allowed a smaller rig. It was a process of lightening everything as much as possible, and the final result was a boat that is potentially the fastest we have built to date.

Andy and I chopped out and assembled the timbers as usual. Once we started to heave the full frames astride the keel, it

quickly became apparent that *Tallulah* was going to be a sweet shape. Starting four stations back from the stem and working aft, we set up all the frames until arriving four stations short of the sternpost. This was quickly done, all erected in a matter of days. From here aft it would be half frames, not traversing the centre line, fastened to the sides of the deadwood.

Before these are set into place the counter must be assembled. This I should describe in some detail, as it is the one part of a wooden boat that people seem to have trouble visualising (see page 99). Firstly, the horn timbers are set up on each side of the sternpost. These project aft, rising upwards past the deck

Tallulah's counter is framed up with the fashion-piece-yoke in the foreground and further aft, across at what will be deck level, is the arch-board.

level finishing at what will be the taff-rail, so giving the vessel its full length and forming a backbone to the counter. Getting these 14 feet long heavy lumps of oak into place is precarious. Until fastened they float around overhead in mid air, yet ultimately must be positioned to within a quarter of an inch, both vertically and horizontally. They define the whole profile of the vessel; the length of counter and deck level. Even the slightest change of pitch changes everything. I've seen people

Lowering the full frames into place, Andy cuts back the floors to fit over the keel

The crew take a well-earned break, a cup of tea in the sun.

Jim Bob holding the half model, with Andy beside him.

looking on in disbelief at me balanced on a barrel trying to measure an invisible point in thin air above my head, unaware that I have several plumb-bobs hanging and strings taut on the horizontal as reference points.

Once the horn timbers are thoroughly fastened through the deadwood it is time to drop in the fashion-piece-yoke, a slab of oak that straddles the horn timbers on the foreside of the sternpost. This defines the shape of the hull at this point and will carry much of the weight. We then move aft to the knuckle in the horn-timbers where the deck level will be. Here an arch-board is placed, traversing the boat, and laid over the horn-timbers, giving the full beam of the counter and support to the middle and outer quarter timbers.

These quarter timbers are dropped in from above. At the inboard end, they butt against the fashion-piece-yoke, further aft they notch over the arch-board as they carry on up to finish at the taff-rail. We now have the main structure of the counter. To finish, all it needs is blocking in with noggins athwart-ships, thus giving landing for the planking and filling out the curves. The counter is at this stage self-supporting but should still be braced to prevent racking whilst planking. Ribbons are nailed about the boat to stiffen it. After this we can move back to fitting the half frames that are now dropped into her belly, filling the gap from the full frames and the counter. Once all this is completed, we have a boat that just needs a little finishing!

Victor took a strong interest in *Tallulah's* structure and followed our progress, often phoning to check that a certain part of the boat had been done in the correct way. I didn't mind. It showed he understood and appreciated the effort that goes into making a good boat. Once I was pouring hot pitch into the counter framing, an important job, to eliminate any chance of water getting trapped and so causing rot, when Victor rang. With a hot ladle in one hand and phone in the other, Victor asked if we would pitch the counter. To which I teasingly replied that it would be a complete waste of time.

The build of each boat is very much a partnership between the owners and myself. It's impossible to work with an owner you don't like. I have been very lucky in that they all have been good people. One friend, a prolific builder of utilitarian hard chine metal boats of a philistine nature for the DIY market, once told me scare stories of customers

The clutter of a boatyard but from it all, beauty rises. **Above:** *Planking nearly completed.* **Below:** *Andy laying the deck.*

ripping him off. 'Beware,' he warned me. 'Never trust the sods.' All my customers have become good friends. I have a theory that beautiful boats only attract beautiful people and touch wood this has so far proven true.

Victor and Ann Marie had a clear idea of what they wanted for their interior fit-out. Time was spent sourcing obscure items such as handmade French copper sinks, bronze taps from Bulgaria and light fittings from Mongolia! They also wanted extra little details to the woodwork, such as carving barley-twist to the compression posts and *Tallulah's* name carved on the transit rail. For them beauty is in the detail, which reminded me of how seduced I was by my first impressions aboard *Charmian*. The details in the woodwork show a confidence, not in just building a boat but in doing so with ease. The difference

between the accomplished and the struggling is in subtle decorative details. I don't mean superfluous decoration, but knowing when to add beading to the stanchions to diminish their visual weight.

Morale was good. Andy, Jim, Jonny and Nick the new painter were all happy and working well. After the traumas that had befallen me during the build of *Ezra* – the divorce from Sara, sailing *Agnes* back from the US, my near annihilation by the tax man – I now felt much more in control of my destiny. Living aboard *Agnes* had sharply reduced my domestic overheads. Running the business on my own gave me a more joined-up understanding of all its aspects. I was even starting to get an idea of the real costs of building a boat and that all-important detail, cash flow! I was solvent and my

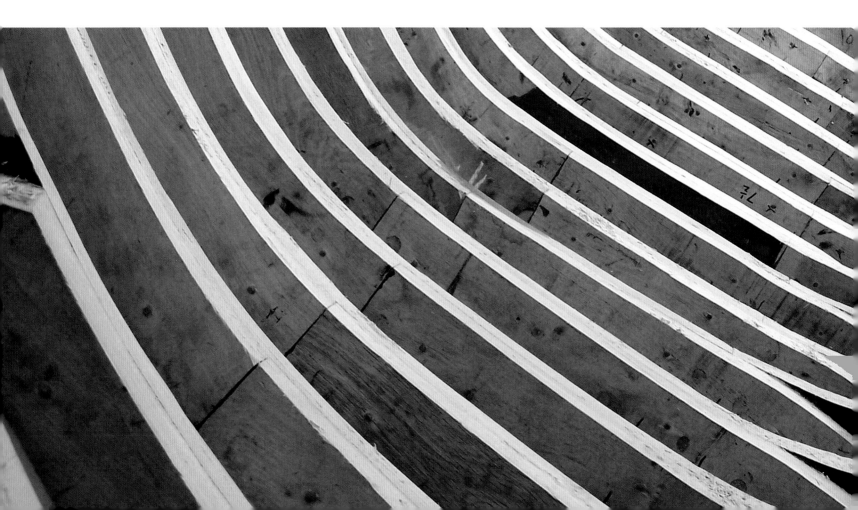

bachelor life aboard *Agnes* was proving pleasant. Tied up alongside a trendy wine bar, I only needed to be twenty again and all would be paradise. With the New Year came thoughts of the pending launch, the date was set for April 11 2008, it was time to think of the sails.

In the quest for a lighter rig I was having discussions with our trusty sailmaker, the inimitable Patrick Selman. With his neat silver beard, Patrick is an old and trusted friend and has been making sails for me as long as I can remember. His loft lies under a railway arch near the docks in Falmouth. Of the old school, he works on instinct and rule of thumb; very much a man after my own heart. Some view him as a bit of a roughish pirate, definitely a more colourful character than most men. Patrick started out building then working a sailing oyster

boat, dredging under sail in the winters and then racing in the summer. He made the first sails for his own boat, and such was his success racing that he developed a summer trade in sailmaking whilst still dredging for oysters in winter.

Now many years on, we sat in Patrick's loft discussing *Tallulah's* sails. I had to tread carefully. 'I don't bloody well tell you how to make boats, so don't tell me how to make sodding sails,' said Patrick. His sails are as tough as man can make. The heavy cloth used in *Agnes's* mainsail was meant for square-riggers, cut with narrow vertical seams, thick bolt ropes, and all hand-sown with old fashioned roped cringles spliced and driven home with a large mallet. This beautiful piece of craftsmanship saved our lives when hove-to in the dark wastes of the Atlantic.

The sails for *Ezra* were also heavily built. 'I like Sam,' reasoned Patrick, 'and it blows hard up there in Scotland.' His ethos was 'make them tough and strong like the boats.' Yet there I was sat on a bolt of cloth in the sail loft suggesting that for *Tallulah* we make things a little lighter. 'Bollocks! You going soft on me!' After a moment's reflection I came up with a plan. 'Fancy a pint of Doom Bar down the Chain Locker?' Four pints in and we were starting to make progress. After eight we were hugging each other and in agreement to use a lighter cloth, with a flatter cut. Finally we staggered home to sleep it off, a good day done.

Meanwhile Jonny served and spliced *Tallulah's* rigging, while Nick finished painting the interior. The electrician and plumber scrabbled over each other, drilling holes in what seemed like every bulkhead, threading pipes and wires. With the standing rigging set up it was time to get the topmast and spars aboard the boat. It is always a good moment seeing the rig come together, as suddenly stepping back the boat looks tall and proud. A few days before launching Patrick arrived with the mainsail. We bent it on, set it for a good look. Patrick told me that the rest of the sails would follow. Victor and Ann Marie arrived, excited to see the almost complete *Tallulah*, although Victor looked a little anxious after having been to the sail loft and seen Patrick with yards of cut cloth still strewn across the floor. I reassured him that Patrick always works to the wire and had never let me down yet; he just likes to live on the edge!

The painting finished, *Tallulah* was moved over to the crane berth ready for launching. The spirited seamstress Carla

Left: Tallulah *is framed, faired and planked. The hull is now ready for the fit out.*

Ann Marie stepped aboard, nervous at being the centre of attention. She blessed the vessel with a libation of red wine upon *Tallulah's* stem, whereupon we all cheered. Clive of the yard came and patted Victor on the back; 'Looks like we have a floater this time.'

Next day at six on the early flood tide the mist hung in the wooded valley. We were all aboard with the engine purring, ready to cast off and head downriver before the tide ebbed, but there were still no headsails. Patrick always cuts it fine, but I was disappointed, knowing that we would have to put to sea under mainsail alone. *Tallulah* moved forward, pulling away from the quay when with a sudden thud a sail

Adams arrived with the cushions and suddenly the boat looked beautifully finished. It is always amazing how the soft furnishings suddenly change things. They set the whole vessel aglow, bringing out the lustre of the varnish-work.

Tallulah was ready and with the crane taking the strain, slowly she lifted up and out of the cradle into the sky above. Click, click went the cameras as she was swung out over the water. Faces looked up anxiously, worried at her being so high, then down she gently went, until the heel of her keel kissed the surface, down further, parting the water as she settled into her element. The strops went slack and she finally moved of her own accord.

This is always the moment when a wave of emotion comes over me, and I think it gets worse every time.

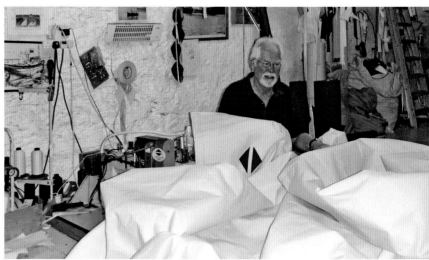

Above: *Patrick Selman in his sail loft under a railway arch in Falmouth tussling with billowing clouds of sails.*

Left: *At his trade, Jonny the rigger, sweet deadeyes and neat work to be sure.*

Top left: Tallulah *out of the shed and ready to launch, whilst the next boat is already taking shape.*

Facing page: *First sea trials in Falmouth Bay.*

bag landed on the deck. I turned around just in time to dodge another bag flying high through the air. There was Patrick with a beaming grin. 'Never missed it yet!' he shouted, adding 'What are you waiting for. Get the sails up. Shake a leg!' Downriver we went in the still misty morning. Soon the sails were up and *Tallulah* lifted to the first of the Atlantic swell.

The wind stiffened as we cleared the headland. Friends, specks in the meadows above, waved us off. The wind came out of the east, it was a beat to windward but without flinching *Tallulah* came into her stride and away she went, stretching her legs hard on the wind. The mainsail was tight as a drum. The headsails were drawing nicely, the sheets straining. 'We've got one here, she's a good'n,' said I.

Tallulah crossed Falmouth Bay with such a sense of purpose that we quickly arrived off Carrick Roads, passing in under Pendennis Castle. Looking at the log I could not believe that she was doing nine and half knots. We weren't even trying: it must be the tide, I thought. Disbelievingly, I turned her about to see how she would do in the other tack. Away she leapt undeterred on her new course, now doing ten knots! Well this was a slippery girl indeed! It just shows that it is the balance of all the elements that is important – a good hull, a balanced rig, well-cut sails and someone that knows how to drive it all. Exhilarated by the sheer speed, we tacked again and headed for home. I couldn't wait to get back to my drawing board and sketch out ideas for a 60 foot version of *Tallulah*. Now that would be a fine thing!

Above: Tallulah's *spacious interior finished in oak and painted paneling.* **Below:** *Alongside* Tallulah *is her sister* Lizzie May.

Above & below: *Putting* Tallulah *through her sea trials on a day of cloud and threatening rain, but she was happy in her new task.*

Amelie Rose *on her first sail with the proud Nick Beck at the rail aft, Jonny Albrecht at the helm, William Collinson and Arne Maynard are on the deck.*

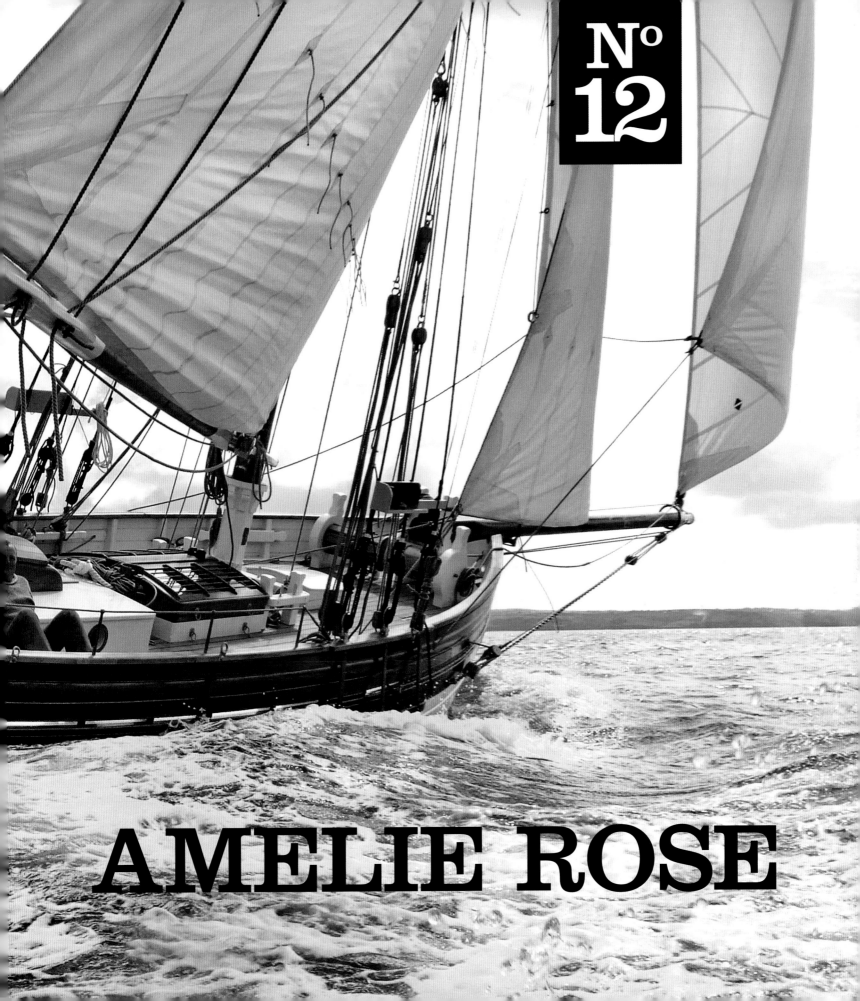

AMELIE ROSE

Andy cutting up slabs of oak, roughing out the frames, and following the chalk marks that I have drawn on the appropriate bend.

When finishing a new boat there is always a great sigh of relief at seeing one's labours complete and, on launch day, stepping back to appreciate how she stands up out there amongst the others.

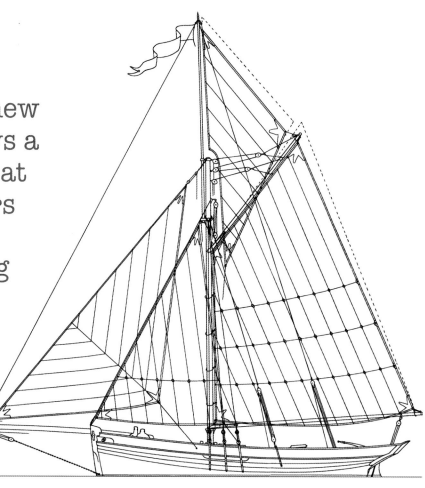

Some years ago a young couple named Nick Beck and Melisa Collett sailed into Falmouth on a twenty odd foot little plastic thing from the Solent. It was a lovely spring day and *Agnes* happened to be anchored off the town quay. Being curious, Nick rowed over and asked if they could come aboard. Such was their interest I felt it only polite to invite them along for a sail that afternoon. Stepping ashore later that day, the dye was cast, Nick and Melisa were determined that one day they would own a pilot cutter of their own.

They both worked in the City and wanted out. I invited them to sail with us at the end of the month in the Pilot Cutter Championships and so we became good friends. Some time after this and despite seeing all our antics at the races,

Left: *Lofting out and getting a fair curve with the batten.*

Facing page top: *Andy assembling a frame on the lofting floor.*
Bottom: *Bagmill Ben is planing up* Amelie Rose's *keel while Andy is cutting out the stem with a chainsaw.*

Left: *Having assembled* Amelie Rose's *centre line, we now work on the through fastenings. Note the frames stacked upside down.*

they announced that they wished to commission a new vessel, to which I reluctantly agreed. She was to be named *Amelie Rose*, and was to be a sister ship to *Ezra*, our fifth vessel, and they planned to work her in charter out of Poole in Dorset.

Undertaking any new project is always a daunting prospect, as you are totally consumed by it for the best part of two years. So with this in mind one needs to take a deep breath and show a touch of reluctance.

By the spring of 2008 we already had the timbers for this new cutter, the seventh from our ramshackle shed. I had taken templates from the lofting floor that gave the shape from each section of the body plan, then chalked these onto the slabs of oak that were scattered about the yard. Whereupon Andy stoically hacked away with the chainsaw, working his way methodically through this massive pile of strewn oak. Within two weeks we had converted this jumble into a neat stack of frames ready for the thicknesser.

By the time that *Tallulah* was ready to sail away we had *Amelie Rose* framed up. It takes eight weeks to loft and frame the main structure of the hull, including the counter. Then it was on to the planking; a couple of weeks to sort out the sheer strake, scarf and fair it in. After that, with two shipwrights working, it took eleven weeks to plank her up. Job done, a 44 footer in five and a bit months!

With so much going on, our good friend Bagmill Ben said he could give us a few months helping Andy. Ben is as keen as mustard, having grown up working on a West Country trading ketch called *Irene*. They worked well together, Andy with the knowledge and Ben the drive. Since the previous autumn we had always been a man down, as Jim had sailed off to the Caribbean in his tiny gaffer in search of adventure and fortune. So with Ben not being with us for long, it was time to recruit another shipwright. I needed a good man to fit all the deck beams. The intention was to finish the covering-board, stations, lodging-knees, Samson-post and all the deck structure before August. Then in the summer heat the deck could be laid and left to settle while we were away sailing.

The issue of a work force is always a thorny one. How do you get good people worth their salt? I need skilled woodworkers,

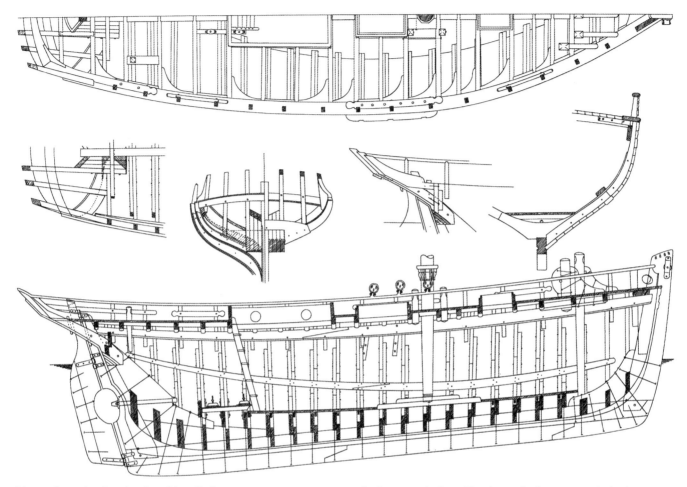

Above: *A construction drawing of* Amelie Rose.

Facing page:*Andy and Ben lower the frames onto the keel.*

ones with a sense of rhythm and speed, that have spent long enough being self employed to know that a job is priced and has to come within budget. Part of being a good shipwright is understanding what is relevant to the job in hand and not getting wrapped up in detail. With boatbuilding the level to which you work changes with the size of the vessel. A little yacht must be chiseled but a three masted schooner must be hacked. Also the level of finish depends on which part of the boat you are working on, from framing-up to making skylights. Different disciplines are required to tackle the different tasks, one must adapt to the respective stages in the boat's construction. Too often I have seen someone cautiously nibbling away at frames with a spoke-shave when they should be using a tar planer. One has got to be sensible and keep a holistic view, the right attitude and tool for the job is imperative.

Once one has found a good boatbuilder it is as hard to retain them. Many are young and footloose, as I once was, always moving on in search of pastures new. A good example of the restless shipwright is our Jim Bob. If I could put together a team of a dozen guys like him I could build the *Cutty Sark* in a trifle. To replace him I foolishly took on someone for the purposes of this book I will call Rupert, a fine example of the problem in our industry today. Traditional boatbuilding is no longer a downtrodden profession but has become a noble craft, populated by an influx of gentleman boatbuilders with a private school education, what someone once labelled the 'educated artisan'. Rupert was a typical example. He had done forestry in Wales, some timber-framing, built green oak barns, and was now trying his hand at boatbuilding.

A soft-spoken chap with a well kept genteel beard, I took to Rupert immediately, agreeing that he could start on Monday. I soon discovered my mistake. Rupert was not used to working at an industrial pace and did not want to be rushed. In effect we had someone with family money who was just not hungry enough, he was playing at making things whilst ambling about with the inherent arrogance of privilege, thinking he could set his own agenda. Rupert had acquired the habit of wearing a leather jerkin hung with an array of obsolete tools and did everything, even the smallest job, with a massive slick (a large chisel with a 4 inch cutting edge that looked like a spade, with a handle as long!). I watched in disbelief as he struggled to cut a 2 inch dovetail into the hard opepe carlins. Finally I had to say something, he was just taking too long on the job. It was too painful to watch, I could not take it any longer. I cajoled him to try a more sensible sized chisel, but indignantly he challenged me to a duel –

who could cut a dovetail the quickest. He with his spade or me with an inch chisel. Needless to say he did not stay with us long.

Over the years I have developed a reliable way of assessing the merits of any new employee. Not by looking at their portfolio, but by asking them to walk across the yard to the toilet. It is all told in the way a man walks: some hurry, eager to get there; others slouch, as if dragging their limbs, not wanting to arrive. Attitude is everything, the rest can be taught. A good craftsman with a resistant attitude and slow metabolism is no use to man nor beast.

The most difficult part of building boats is being an employer. I was beginning to tire of being in charge of others and their foibles and thinking instead of having a break from it all. It had been a long road and I needed a rest. For several years I had toyed with the direction in which to take the business,

Left: *Andy planking up the transom.* **Below right:** *Nick peers through the framing of his new boat. Joanna amused at our antics.*

Steaming in full swing. Andy is taping up a leak in the plastic sausage inflated over the plank.

should it expand or contract? After much deliberation I had a Eureka moment. Realising that the only way forward was to take back control of my life, I decided to shut down the business, to walk away before I was carried out in a box. I still wanted to build boats but needed to reflect on my future and catch up on other things.

All at once I could feel the weight lifting from my shoulders. I could see the way forward, a life of my own, rather than constantly dealing with the egos of others. If there had been someone to share the burden, says a business partner, I would have continued. But it seems there are two types

Above: *The deck is now laid and paid with stanchions dropped in.*
Left & bellow: *Bulwarks on and looking complete. The rudder-post is in but no blade as yet.*

Facing page: *Andy starts to lay the sole, a lot of joggling and notching in around the frames.*

Irish Sea, but my reward from South Wales was a new love, Joanna Willcox, a lovely, sweet girl and the kindest lass you could ever wish to meet. She hailed from Cardigan and was the captain of a Manx lugger. She could tie a bowline behind her back with one hand and had no fear of hardship afloat in old wooden boats. We had met several years before at a boat festival in France and although nothing came of it, I had always held a candle for her. Now many years on, her life had changed and she helped me sail *Agnes* back home to Cornwall. Two years later I asked her to be my wife, but that's another story!

of people in the world – followers or leaders, those who shy away from responsibility and are happiest as employees, or those capable of sharing the burden but would rather go off to do their own thing. With all this in mind I went sailing on *Agnes*, first to Brittany then up the Irish Sea to the Isle of Man, leaving Andy and Nick to valiantly carry on with laying the deck of *Amelie Rose*.

It felt good to be off seeking adventure, away into the eye of the storm, doing battle with the elements. It just so happened that the summer of 2008 was one of the wettest and windiest ever, and I eventually limped back to Falmouth with a broken rig, the bowsprit and topmast swept away by a big lump of the

On returning to the yard it was good to see how *Amelie Rose* had progressed. Andy had done well, perhaps I was not needed after all, but for the moment it was back to work on the interior and the start of the final fit out. We were on a countdown to the launch. This is when I made my earth-shattering announcement. We were finishing work once *Amelie Rose* was launched. No more boats to build. The lads were stunned at this, but said nothing. Although I could see they were hurt at my decision, I was adamant.

This was a strange time. We were all eager to see *Amelie Rose* launched yet there was a reluctance to bring an end to employment. I struggled to maintain the momentum and get *Amelie Rose* finished on time and on budget. No boat built by

Working Sail had been late in the water and I did not want this one to be any different. The date of the launch, 24 April 2009, was dictated by the tides that would take her downriver. It is only the equinoctial tides that make it possible, so the date had been set when the keel was laid. But spirits were low and I was working late into the evenings in an attempt to keep to the schedule.

At this time, Jim Bob came back to England. He had been shipwrecked off Morocco on his way to the Caribbean. His sweet little gaffer had been stoved-in and foundered some seventy miles offshore. Luckily a passing coaster plucked him from the sea and put him ashore in Portugal, shaken but glad to be alive! He returned home to lick his

wounds, but undaunted he announced that he had found a replacement boat in Portugal and now needed money to get it sorted. I offered him some much-needed work and so here he was back at the yard. Jim's arrival gave new energy to the flagging team. He started on making the spars while Andy worked through the cabins, and I fitted the engine and tanks. Then the next stage came and the electronics. Every day more boxes arrived. John Andrew, the electrician, mopped his brow with mental fatigue, overwhelmed at all that was wanted.

Launch day arrived with a mad frenzy aboard. Andy was still fitting chocks on the coach roof for the dinghy, Jon serving the rigging, Nick screwing down deck fillers and me running around doing all the odd jobs nobody else wanted to do. The crane poised overhead, the yard workers swarmed aboard to attach the strops.

I had to call a retreat: 'Ok that's it boys – everyone off.'

Top right: *Jonny working aloft. All the running rigging is yet to be roved.* **Below:** *The carving on the badge-boards is picked out and all the rigging roved.*

As the crane took the weight and *Amelie Rose* swung high up over the cradle that was to transport her down the yard, up popped a disconcerted electrician from the hatch. 'What's happening?' 'Get back in there. There's no time to stop. We're sailing tomorrow!'

Knowing that this would be the last boat for some time I decided to invite all the friends and locals I could think of as a thank you for their support over the years. Joanna, who had newly moved down to Cornwall, helped me set out benches and tables for the good spread that was laid on by Oona, my stepdaughter, along with plenty of wine and barrels of beer. The vicar of St Mawes came and gave a blessing to our good vessel. All those on the quay jumped aboard for a photo shoot, squeezing in like sardines with no room to spare. The vicar announced that Jesus was amongst us and we raised our glasses in a toast to the good ship *Amelie Rose*. The food was eaten and drink consumed, evening came

Below: *The rogues gallery. Amelie Rose's launch day and a gang of friends have climbed aboard for the camera.* **Below right:** *Our sailing vicar Ken Boullier blesses the boat, while we listen on, I one side and Melisa and Nick the other.*

and slowly the gathering broke up and everyone but the diehards round the beer barrel wended their way home.

Next morning it was cold and wet but the tide was high and it was time to leave the quay. *Amelie Rose* slid downriver in search of the sea. As the day strengthened, so did a cold wind and by midday we were tied up in Falmouth. To warm ourselves we retreated to the fireside of the good old Chain Locker and a few pints of Doom Bar were placed on the table to celebrate.

Over the next week or so I sorted out the final tweaks and adjustments to the rig and finished the painting. Nick and Melisa familiarised themselves with their new boat and John the electrician tweaked things down below with the multitude of gadgets. But in truth I was happy to potter. Back in the yard all was quiet, although it did take some time for the boys to adapt.

Facing page top & above : *Putting Amelie Rose through her paces in Falmouth harbour.* **Facing page below left:** Amelie Rose *is all finished, cushions are in and the clock is wound, she has a homely glow.* **B**elow right: *Tied up at Falmouth after* Amelie Rose's *maiden voyage from Gweek.*

Every morning Andy would stand at the shed, rolling a cigarette, wondering where everyone was, automatically drawn there after so many years of routine. We had worked together for a long time, but it was time for a change and we all had to move on. I suppose it was easier for me as I had made the decision to stop. I was already planning my next move and knew that I would soon be away with Joanna, free on the good ship *Agnes*.

Finally, Nick and Melisa were confident in their ability to sail *Amelie Rose*. We shook hands and I wished them *bon voyage*. Bravely, they had decided to sail alone as a couple without a deckhand to help. I understood how they felt, their wish to be free and at sea on their own boat – just the two of them

and their new life. It would be one of those never-to-forget moments. So with *Amelie Rose* safely away, my own new life could start. Happy times lay ahead, and I had a good woman to share them with.

On the day we launched *Amelie Rose* I went back to the shed to put away the tools and tins of paint and close up the doors. It was time to spend a quiet moment reflecting on all we had achieved over the years. Standing there in the twilight listening to the evening silence, the rooks roosting in the high trees up the valley and the far off sound of laughter around the beer barrels as those gathered for the launch drained the last drop, the stillness was golden. I turned the key in the lock and placed it in my pocket, it was done.

A parade of sail, heading down to the lower mark, in the line up are; Artaius, Amelie Rose, Eve, Mascotte, Annabel J *and* Hesper, *with ahead of them* Cornubia *and already around the mark,* Freja.

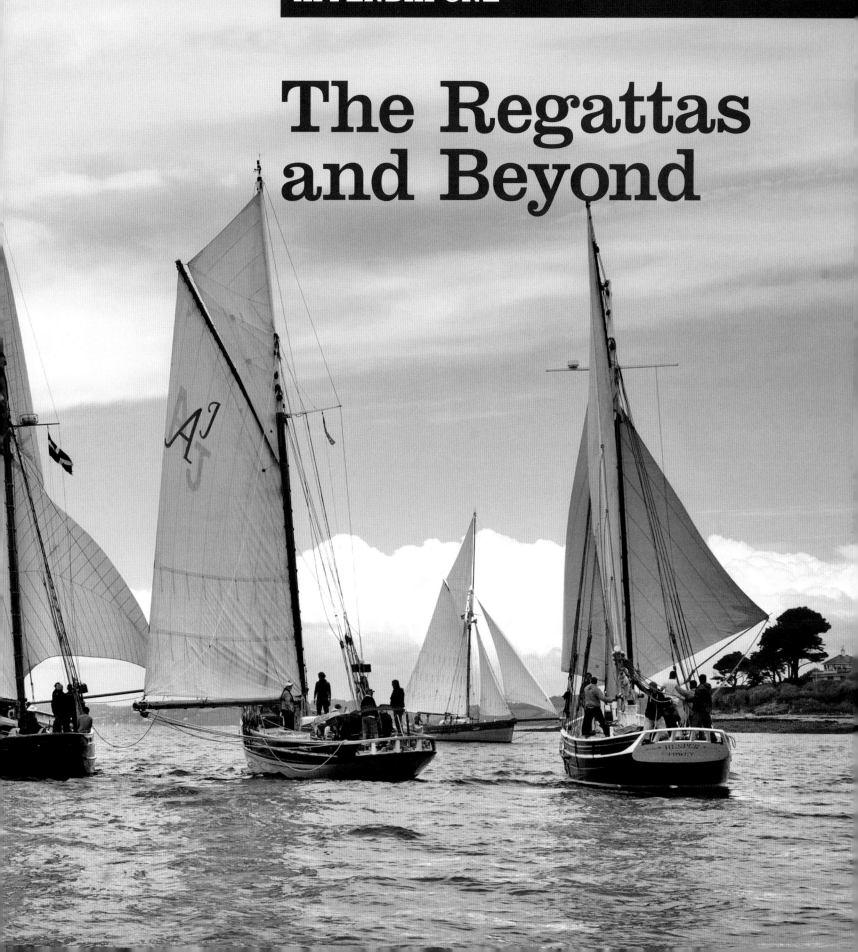

The Regattas and Beyond

This would be a forum for real boats, a moment to shine a light on what we do.

A stiff breeze and Hesper *is working hard to keep ahead of* Mascotte.

On England's East Coast the maritime past has remained vibrant and alive. There is a still a working community of people involved with traditional sail. When I moved to the West Country in 1990 I was saddened to see how little was left. None of the great West Country trading schooners had survived, save the solitary *Kathleen & May*. Those in the tough North Atlantic cod trade, the slate trade to the Baltic, the china clay schooners from Par, and, the finest of them all, the schooners of Fowey that sailed to the Azores to bring back citrus fruits – are all no more. Nothing bar three lonely ketches that used to work the Irish Sea, and the little Falmouth oyster boats, these are all that is left.

Despite my initial pessimism, I gradually got to know the handful of people keeping these last embers of knowledge alive, each quietly pursuing their particular passion. Great mentors like Basil Greenhill and David McGregor, who had documented the last years of the schooners. Those who kept the last ketches sailing, including the wonderfully eccentric Leslie Morrish and the lovely Nikki Alford. Perhaps the most numerous of vessels to have survived are the Bristol Channel pilot cutters, such as *Peggy* owned by the sagacious Diccon and Jan Pridie. A rare crossover from east to west is Tony Winter, who started by saving Thames sailing barges and Whitstable oyster smacks before switching his efforts to Bristol Channel pilot cutters, like *Mascotte* and *Cornubia*.

At rest after the race, Freja *is alongside* Hesper *with* Marguerite *anchored behind.*

In the last couple of decades, certain characters have helped a resurgence of interest in traditional boats. Up the Falmouth River, the indomitable Ralf Bird has encouraged a renaissance of the pilot gig. Thanks to him, there are now over 100 regularly racing around Cornwall. Another vessel that twenty years ago was almost totally extinct is the Cornish lugger, which has now come back to life with the help of the great storyteller Paul Greenwood and his Looe Lugger Regattas. Even the Falmouth oyster boats needed help to survive the dark years, largely thanks to Terry Heard followed by his charismatic son Martin.

There have been others as well, those inspired by their affection for regional boats and not giving a damn for conventional thinking, who have battled away up muddy creeks in an effort to keep our old historic vessels alive and still sailing.

Through the wonderful Alf Jenkins I too had embarked on a cause, to resurrect the Scillonian pilot cutter. From the start I dreamed of the day when there would be enough of them to make it possible for an annual race, a showcase for these boats. By the spring of 2006, with **Agnes** back sailing in Cornwall under my command, and *Ezra* newly launched, we suddenly had five vessels afloat. If we could also entice a few Bristol boats down and the odd Le Havre cutter then we would have a big enough fleet to put on a regatta. It would be great to get the original cutters sailing alongside the replicas, building friendships, and hopefully bringing a new energy to it all.

For some years I had proposed this idea, as I felt that regattas were a good way to increase interest in traditional boats. But in the meantime I was too busy building boats to do much. Finally Adam and Debbie Purser of *Eve* came to the rescue, picking up the torch and setting up the Pilot Cutter Championship. As *Eve* was based in St Mawes it was the logical venue. In its heyday St Mawes had been a stronghold of pilot cutters so it felt appropriate. Today it remains a picturesque Cornish harbour lodged behind the eastern peninsular of Falmouth Bay. The anchorage is in deep water, if somewhat open to the west. The fetch is rarely bad, as the Lizard peninsular blocks the Atlantic by two leagues to the west; so in all, a good place, easy to sail into, and more importantly, a free anchorage.

Falmouth, just across the water, would have been the ideal host. For years it had been the home of the Classics Race. But sadly this event has been in decline, in my opinion due in no small measure to the Falmouth Harbour Commissioners and their constant demands for money. In 1990 when I first raced in the Falmouth Classics, it was well frequented by all manner of large vessels from far afield, particularly the French. Because of the hospitality the French lavish on us we were eager to make them welcome here, but I hold my head in shame at the way they are treated. How many times have I seen a vessel sail into the anchorage, often after a long and hazardous voyage, to be welcomed by the harbour launch, not with a cheerful 'Welcome to Falmouth' but a gruff 'Once you're anchored we need you to pay.' Even if they drop anchor in the middle of the night, at eight sharp the harbour launch comes alongside with a bump and 'Wake up! You can't stay here without paying.'

I blame this attitude on the Thatcherite policy of making the Commissioners responsible for their own finance. Now it is all about profiting from what should be a free anchorage. I accept the need to charge for the use of moorings, but the anchorage should be free to visiting sailors. I can hear them say, 'Some one has to pay,' but why, what's wrong with free short stay parking? Surely the Harbour Commissioners should be financed by the state not by a few yachtsman.

The French that used to visit with their beautiful wooden vessels, don't anymore, too shocked by this meanness of spirit. Falmouth Classics could have been another Douarnenez, but instead has dwindled away to nothing. What could have grown and become great for the town, bringing business to the shops and civic pride to all, has been killed through petty bureaucratic small mindedness.

So Adam and Debbie, with the enlightened support of the St Mawes Harbour Master and the people of that fine village, put together a plan to create the 'Pilot Cutter Championship'. Adam sent out brochures and forms to all he could think of, contacting any friend with a relevant vessel. We were all invited and delighted to participate. This would be a forum for real boats, a moment to shine a light on what we do. Also, I had long wanted to test my boats against others. Observing them competing would be enlightening to me as a designer, teaching me how to get the best out of them and hopefully improve their performance, particularly in the rig.

This I had seen happen with the spritsail barges on the East Coast. Thanks to a revival in racing, the bowsprit class came back into existence in the late 1970s and the overall sailing qualities of the barges improved.

The first gathering at St Mawes was on a lovely warm summer's day in June 2006. The sea was flat with a hot hazy sun and the gentlest of winds. We were a small gathering of just four cutters plus Nikki Alford's trading ketch *Bessie Ellen*. The line up was *Eve* sailed by Debbie, *Lizzie May* sailed by Jonny our rigger for the owner Simon Bell, *Agnes* with me, and the famous French cutter *Jolie Brise* skippered by Toby Mariss. The first leg of the race was out to *Bessie Ellen*, as if we were putting a pilot aboard, then away over to Trefusis Point near Flushing, before heading back to St Mawes.

To give the slower boats a fighting chance Adam set us a staggered start from anchor, with the fast *Jolie Brise* waiting till last. We were allowed to set the mainsail but the anchor had to be down and everyone aft of the mast. In the light airs *Eve* was first away, gently gathering way as she passed under our stern to a hail of derision from our motley crew. Next was *Lizzie May*, but before we were aware of what was happening Jonny dived into the sea and swam across to *Agnes* towing a bucket in an attempt to secure its lanyard to our propeller. There was a great ruckus, a lot of prodding with oars and boathooks. I hung over the side in an attempt to stop the sabotage. In the end Jonny had to retreat. *Lizzie May* was gathering speed. Jonny chased after her and was dragged battered and bruised from the sea. Shaking my fist and shouting 'We'll have you!' it was our turn to go. 'Run out the jib, cast off, let's get them!' Away we went, gathering pace. Although on deck it appeared busy – running up the topmast jib, setting the main tops'l and sheeting out the main, *Agnes* seemed to be moving in slow motion, as the gentlest of breezes carried us at little more than two knots. I glanced behind to see *Jolie Brise* hard on our tail. 'Heck, we had better work at this.'

I have always liked this type of racing, with the handicaps dealt out at the beginning. From then on it's a straight race. The fast boats chase the slow ones in the hope that it's a close call at the finish. As you overhaul one of the other boats there is also a chance to pelt them with whatever comes to hand! The race progressed but the wind stayed light and fickle, just a gentle breeze coming in patches that caused one boat to pull ahead and then the next. We worked hard to keep *Jolie Brise* behind as long as possible. Once round *Bessie Ellen* we bore away, first catching *Eve* and then *Lizzie May*. We were doing well,

Above: Hesper *leads the fleet with* Pegasus *behind.* **Below:** *Sailing hard.* Agnes *in pursuit of* Jolie Brise *and* Mascotte. *I'm at the helm with Dylan sat close by.*

even holding out against *Jolie Brise*, but then came the windward leg and what a sight we had as *Jolie Brise* came into her own. We were going tack for tack but the sails that *Jolie Brise* now set took my breath away. The luff of her Yankee extended from the top of the topmast to the end of the bowsprit, not an inch wasted. With that kind of power we didn't stand a chance, but it was an honour to be whipped by such a boat. This had been a good first Championship, we all had reason to be proud, and looked forward to a bigger turnout the following year.

By June 2007 and the second Pilot Cutter Championship word had got out and a fine crowd of eleven cutters assembled: *Agnes, Alpha, Annabel J, Charmian, Eve, Hesper, Lizzie May, Marguerite, Mascotte, Peggy,* and *Velsia*. It was great to see them all anchored in St Mawes Bay, a sight to warm even the most philistine of hearts, and five of them were my own boats. I had never before seen them all together in one place. All those planks shaped and fastenings driven home. All that blood, sweat and tears. It felt a worthy cause. Again the weather was light and beautifully sunny.

The second Pilot Cutter Championship. Word had got out and a fine crowd of eleven cutters assembled. Here the first boats are rounding the outer mark, from left to right: Lizzie May, Alpha, Hesper, Marguerite, Eve *and* Agnes.

I was pleased to see *Charmian* amongst us; it had been a long time since I had walked away from her at Southampton, hurt at the loss. A lot of water had passed under the bridge. I felt like an ex-lover not quite knowing how to deal with the situation. But she was fine and much loved by her new master Les Arkell, who was sailing her faster than I had ever managed. Anyway I too had a new love – *Agnes*!

The two days of racing were a sight to see. As the fleet spread out from the start line, we filled the horizon with our wooden cutters, no plastic, just us. The first leg to the outer

mark was followed by a turn east to windward for the second mark before a final tack home. The start was good. We were well placed to windward but slowly the boats were drawn inexorably together until halfway out there was a crunch. *Peggy* was to windward and leaned down on us, while Jonny with a load of ruffians on *Lizzie May* was running abreast to leeward about three feet away. Holding his course was William in *Hesper*, ever eager to force the pace, driving up under their lee. We ended up with a sandwich of four cutters, all stealing each other's wind and in a magnetic pull from which we were

Above: *Beating towards the windward mark.* **Below left:** *Jonny is at the helm of Freja and at the rail my good friend and designer of this book, Christian Topf.* **Below right:** *Patrick Selman watching the race aboard Hesper.*

unable to break free. Booms on each others decks, pushing and shoving, banter flying we drove on as one until Diccon Pridie with *Peggy* managed to pull away, leaving us all in his foul wind.

The next day we again got off to a good start, but fell off to leeward, losing ground all the time. I could not work out what was happening. We even had two extra crew aboard, eager and keen to pull ropes in an attempt to get *Agnes* going, but she was sluggish and nothing we did seemed to help. I looked over the taffrail to see if Jonny had tied a bucket to the prop. At the clubhouse prize giving I smiled at the ribbing and had another pint. In the end it was *Hesper* that ended up the overall winner, and deservedly so. Proudly, William and Arne sailed back to Fowey and I took a little vicarious pleasure in their win.

Some weeks later when racing in the Looe Lugger festival I came up against the pilot cutter *Peggy* again. This time, I was determined to learn from the encounter with the shrewd Diccon. We were again neck and neck on a beam reach in light airs. I watched and copied everything he did in order to understand the edge he had. It was a revelation to see how he operated.

Nonchalantly, he and Jan walked about the deck as if at a garden tea party, though instead of tea their cups contained red wine. He would sit on the coaming as if resting his weary limbs whilst surreptitiously easing the mainsheet. Jan leant on the boom as if idly snoozing but in fact she was slyly pushing it out as Diccon eased. Not a word was said, they knew each other so well. It was all very covert but I was not to be fooled. I too eased the sheet. Wherever Diccon went I followed and to my amazement we kept with them all the way. *Peggy* could not shake us off. That is until we chose different tactics and I mistakenly tacked early. Once I was unable to observe his tricks *Peggy* was soon away and gone, we had lost her. But I had seen enough. The penny had dropped.

The Falmouth oystermen who had sailed with us at St Mawes had pinned everything in as much as possible. With our more traditional rigs it's about slackening off. If she's not going well then ease the sheets until she gets in the groove. I know this seems back to front compared with modern yachts but trust me, when next sailing and you are unhappy with your boat, ease the sheets. Part of the problem is that when racing one gets tense and too eager to pull on things. Take a leaf out of Diccon's book, relax and have another sip of red from the teacup.

The following year Alan Reekie, my surrogate father from Iron Wharf in Faversham, sailed with us. Alan had been the skipper

of the champion spritsail barge *Ironsides* in the 1970s. What he didn't know about racing was not worth the knowing and I was eager to absorb all I could. We did well, sailing *Agnes* for the first time with a keen and sober crew. Tactics was the order of the day, putting *Agnes* in places to gain unseen advantage. Alan was mainsheet man, the most important post aboard, from where you see all and can control all. He would rap me with the back of his knuckles, 'OHY, Let's put a board in and get out of this foul air,' and then, 'Sheet her out boys, let the rudder balance.' His guidance was eagerly received; to learn through others is the best way. A few choice words have more wisdom than any amount of studying in textbooks. Racing is the one place where one sees ones mistakes most sharply. Each year I look forward to the challenge and the process of learning through watching and listening. Maybe one day I will know how to do it properly and get the best out of *Agnes*.

In 2009 the rush to finish our latest build had left *Agnes* neglected. After the previous year's exploits in the Irish Sea the wreckage of broken spars, wire and rope still lay on her deck. Now freed from my chains, after the launch of *Amelie Rose* and with the help of Joanna, I felt irresponsible and young again! But it was May and the lack of time before the pilot cutter championship in June meant no topmast. This would leave *Agnes* under-rigged and without much chance of victory in the races, unless it blew hard. But then, the lack of windage aloft, all that standing and running rigging now gone, could give us an advantage. No matter, it is about the taking part not the winning – or so they tell me!

We set sail to meet the other boats at Fowey. Under our reduced rig in a warm southerly I was content just to be with Joanna and coasting along free of the land. 'Sail ahoy!' There far ahead on the starboard bow was what looked like a pilot cutter, but one I could not recognise. As we drew closer, the penny finally dropped: it was *Amelie Rose*. Never having seen her from afar, I did not recognise the boat we had spent the last eighteen months building. As we converged, a great shout of joy went up. They had a charter party aboard and looked like old hands at the job. It was good to see them already slotting into the groove so well, and I must say what a beautiful boat they had!

On arrival at Fowey I was pleased to see *Amelie Rose* sail in without using the engine and bring up alongside without a fuss, very much obligatory in my book. The engine is only for when she is becalmed. I remember back on the barges, old Donald telling me how, as a lad, his skipper had been forced

Launch day at Gweek Quay, Freja is about to take to the water in April 2012. With her proud owners Anders Johnson giving a speech to those gathered and his wife Marion on the other side. Joanna and myself are in the middle, with the sailing vicar Ken Boullier to our left.

to have an engine fitted to his sailing barge. Reluctantly he got used to the infernal thing, but on arriving at any harbour he would turn it off, so that he could handle the vessel safely in under sail.

So what is all this about, all this building and sailing of these boats? It's about holding true to a way of life that has been ours, and our father's before us. It only takes one generation to break the link. *Agnes* is more than just a wooden boat. To me it feels that she is part of a greater force, maintaining the continuity, keeping the candle burning. When I was a boy in Greece rowing about the harbour watching the old sea captain Kapitano Staviros pumping out his old schooner I sensed the poignancy of him at the end of his life and me at the beginning of mine. Without realising it, he handed me the flame to carry forth, so that now when walking the deck of *Agnes* I can sense the echo of his spirit alongside me. I feel a deep belonging when aboard *Agnes*. It feels the right place to be. This is not just a boat, it is a time machine that carries me back to a finer age. One day I too hope that a young lad will find inspiration from the unwitting example that I set and he too will pick up the flame, and so the circle will carry on.

But in the meantime there is much to do, many more boats to build and sail. We need to continue the progress that has been achieved in the last two decades. The building of new wooden boats is vital to the survival of the old boats. If we lose the ability to build boats we also lose the culture and knowledge that preserves the old ones. So nurture these endangered craftsmen, commission new boats and all will be well. I have only built

eight cutters to date, but what I am most proud of is that my example has influenced the building of double that number – with more on the way. All over Cornwall a new generation of boatbuilders has picked up the baton and rolled up its sleeves. In a county that twenty years ago had pretty much given up on its maritime heritage, life has now returned to the Cornish seas.

There are great projects afoot. Jonny, my long time cohort, is building a fast 42 foot two-masted lugger beside my shed at Gweek. At Millbrook there is a 60 foot three-masted lugger underway. What a sight these will be! The next task is to resurrect the great schooners that brought citrus fruits from the Azores. These were the pinnacles of Cornish boatbuilding and nothing will be complete until one is afloat and sailing.

As for me, I want to put my efforts into the building of a type of pilot cutter that is iconic, but which virtually nothing is known about – the Falmouth pilot cutter. This for me is the natural progression from building *Agnes*, a true Scillonian cutter, which was such a leap into the dark, but so rewarding as a piece of resurrected history. I have long chewed over the possibility of building a historically accurate replica of the Falmouth pilot cutter *Vincent*, which at 62 feet 6 inches would be by far my biggest undertaking to date. As always these days, it was Joanna who was the catalyst. One day she said, 'If you want to do it, then don't mess around, just get on with it.' I had the green light! I lay in bed that night unable to sleep with excitement and fear; 'Where would we find the money? No, I'll worry about that when we come to it!' This is the meaning of life; live on the edge and make things count.

At the recent launch of *Freja*, the eighth
cutter to come forth, our resident vicar
Ken Boullier climbed aboard to bless her
and recited a poem by John O'Donohue.
I stood there, at a moment that held
resonance for the future: *Hold nothing
back, learn to find ease in risk.*

In out-of-the-way places of the heart,
Where your thoughts never think to wander,
This beginning has been quietly forming,
Waiting until you were ready to emerge.

For a long time it has watched your desire,
Feeling the emptiness growing inside you,
Noticing how you willed yourself on,
Still unable to leave what you had outgrown.

It watched you play with the seduction of safety,
And the gray promises that sameness whispered,
Heard the waves of turmoil rise the relent,
Wondered would you always live like this.

Then the delight, when your courage kindled,
And out you stepped onto new ground,
A path of plenitude opened before you.

Through your destination is not yet clear,
You can trust the promise of this opening;
Unfurl yourself into the grace of beginning,
That is at one with your self's desire.

Awake your spirit to adventure;
Hold nothing back, learn to find ease in risk,
Soon you will be home in a new rhythm,
For your soul senses the world that awaits you.

Right: *Driving* Agnes *hard, chasing after* Mascotte.

It is 1886. The Atlantic *and the* Presto *are on the beach at St Marys, laid up and for sale. Later they were both sold to pilots from Milford Haven.*

Pilot Cutters of the Isles of Scilly

The cutter Queen was put ashore in 1889 at St Martins and broken up for fence posts. This is the photo that started me dreaming that one day I would build a Scillonian pilot cutter.

Sometimes the Roads would be crowded with as many as two hundred ships at anchor waiting for a fair wind and letters from their owners giving orders to the next port.

Facing page top: *Sometimes Saint Mary's Roads would be crowded with as many as two hundred ships at anchor waiting for orders and a fair wind.* **Facing page bottom:** *An early photo at Tresco of a cutter drying out. And the original Agnes working to windward in choppy seas.*

The cutter Presto *sailing out through St Mary's Sound past a fishing lugger, outward bound to work.*

It was a late December day in the Scillies on the headland of St Agnes. The wind cut to the bone and was cold and sharp against my face. Low clouds scudded by as I stood looking westward, out over the grey sea. It was time to get warm. Retreating to the cottage fireside, I pulled down a book from the shelves, *Shipwrecks of the Isles of Scilly* by Richard Larn. Idly leafing through, I fell on a photograph taken in the 1880s of the pilot cutter *Queen* lying derelict on a beach in St Martins. It was a fine photograph, a beautiful boat. I had to know more.

The Scillies lie 35 miles west of Lands End: an archipelago of small islands, only five of them inhabited, each less than a few miles across. Surrounding these is a moonscape of smaller islands, rocks and reefs that reach out to the west, eager to snatch at incoming ships. Nowadays this place seems remote from the hub of modern life. But in the mid 19th century it stood at the crossroads of the busiest highway in the world, a time when ships were approaching British waters from all four corners of the Empire to feed the furnaces of the Industrial Revolution. If I had then stood on that same St Agnes headland

I'd have seen an horizon dotted with sail, a score or more vessels all in need of a pilot to help guide them into the safety of St Mary's Roads. Here they could do all essential repairs and take on water and fresh food. Sometimes the Roads would be crowded with as many as two hundred ships at anchor waiting for a fair wind and letters from their owners giving orders to the next port. The Scillies were the logical place to wait, for they gave easy access north to St George's Channel, Bristol and Liverpool, or east up the English Channel to Falmouth, Portsmouth, London, and beyond.

Many of these ships were inward bound from the South Atlantic, spending months at sea working their latitudes and taking sun sights. Once far enough north, they would turn 'Easting home', along Latitude 49½ N, heading for land. Once in the Western Approaches, where the sky was often overcast making it difficult to take an accurate reading with a sextant, their captains navigated by estimating the speed, drift, and set of the tide. Finally, when swinging the lead, they could tell by the shale that stuck to the tallow where they were. If the nights were long and stormy, with the prevailing wind

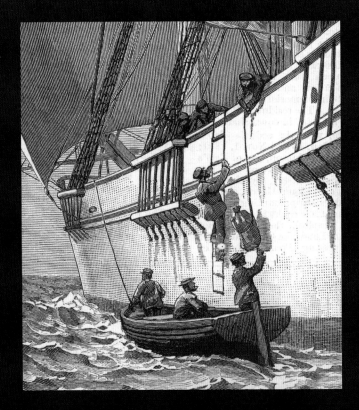

Above: *A pilot climbs aboard a ship from the punt.*
Facing page: *Launching the punt ready to put the pilot aboard.*

As the cutter approaches, its master hails through a speaking trumpet, 'Where you from and where bound?' Master and captain strike terms and agree on the taking of a pilot. The ship backs her main squares and heaves too. The cutter comes close in under the ship's lee and launches her punt, the boy at its oars briskly getting it away before it is dashed to pieces alongside. A pilot is rowed across and smartly heaved aboard by a smiling crew.

This is the first Englishman they have seen for many months, and better still he knows the lie of the land. The squares are braced around and the ship gathers way, heading for land with a new confidence. The cutter, after hauling the punt aboard, would be away west again after another sail on the horizon. All this happened night and day, rain or shine, summer or winter. The greater the wind, the more ships were driven towards these Isles in need of a guiding hand.

Each cutter was operated by a captain and boy, and carried up to eight pilots. In times of abundance even the captain would use his pilotage skills. After helping the lad reef down he would row himself across to the ship, casting the punt adrift as he climbed aboard. This left the lad to sail up to the punt, catch it, and take it in tow before heading home to St Mary's. It wasn't unknown for the boy to be abandoned like this some hundred miles out, to return alone with the cutter. One lad placed a bucket of water by the helm into which he plunged his head in order to stay awake. The 65 foot cutter *Atlantic* came in once, sailed by the boy. Too weak to pick up the mooring-chain he decided to run her up the beach. The spring tide was at its height and the cutter's bowsprit went straight through the window of Bluetts Hotel, knocking the hats off the men standing at the bar before coming to rest.

All cutters had a cargo hold for such things as potatoes, eggs, water, barley, rye, or rope, canvas and spars. Sometimes, revictualling took place far out to sea and payment was made in kind from the ship's cargo. There were also arrangements of 'free trade' with ships from the Far East. The captains of East Indiamen often carried cargo of personal speculation, such as tea or silk, on which an import tax was payable when the goods were landed. Such cargoes were offloaded onto the cutters. An agreement was reached between pilot and captain, which was finally honoured when the captain arrived in port.

briskly pushing in from the southwest, crews grew nervous about the approaching land under their lee. From seaward the Isles of Scilly are low-lying and difficult to pick out. They are guarded by the Western Rocks, ten square miles of treacherous and hidden dangers. Once amongst them, there is no way out. Nowhere in the world have so many ships and men been lost. Every rock marks the death of a sailor. Aboard ship uncertainty kept the lookouts busy.

Whilst still far out to sea, at dawn, on the empty horizon, fine on the starboard bow, a tiny sail is seen in the early light: a pilot cutter. 'Is it? Yes. From where does she hail?' Through the spyglass the captain sees the letter S for Scilly in her sail.

Cutters would regularly go across to Roscoff, where Cornish agents had set up shop. Even the open gigs rowed the 100 miles to France to smuggle back a bale of tobacco and a few casks of brandy. It was said that 'more contraband was landed in Scilly than shipped legally through the Customs & Excise warehouse in the port of London'. However, through the efforts of the preventative force, and the employment of revenue cutters, smuggling declined and was stamped out by the 1840s.

Pilotage in the Scillies flourished throughout the early nineteenth century, shadowing the national boom in the building of sailing ships. The Scillies own fleet was built in the two shipyards on St Mary's. They too played their part in Britain's trade with its Empire, bringing work for the cutters on their return to home waters. This boom for the pilots peaked between the 1830s and 1860s, filling St Mary's Roads with small wooden brigs and barques. The Scillonan pilot was well respected, even by the masters of fine sailing ships. The tea clipper *Thermopylae* employed James Hicks from the cutter *Atlantic*, thus saving many hours at sea and earning her owners a high price for their cargo as the first 'tea of the season'.

Even the tiny island of Samson had two cutters in the days before it was depopulated. This occurred in the 1850s, when its pilots came across a French ship in amongst the Western Rocks. After salvaging her, all Samson's men and boys were taken on board to act as crew for the passage to Plymouth, where a reward was promised. During the night a storm blew up and the ship was lost on Wolf Rock with all hands. This disaster defeated the women's stubborn independence. Unable to fend for themselves, they were forced to abandon the island.

Scillonian pilots traded in some of the harshest conditions known to man. The Atlantic storms pile up on the Continental shelf, causing the seas to run to the most frightening heights. The cutters' moorings were heavy chains salvaged from wrecks. They lay in open bays exposed to certain points of the compass, often rolling heavily in the swell that curls round the islands. In extreme weather the crew laid out 'storm warps'. Heavy ropes were run out to windward and made fast to rocks or headlands, thus taking some of the strain from the mooring chain. The danger of the vessel breaking free and being smashed on the rocks was considerable. Seven out of eleven cutters lost over the years were wrecked in this way rather than at sea.

The cutters would slip their moorings on dark cold January mornings, tacking out through the rocks and reefs straight into the eye of the Atlantic. There was no room for the slightest error. Clawing to windward with the first tinges of dawn, it was vital to gain sea-room. The tearing of canvas or the parting of a rope would be the end of her, as instantly she would be swept onto the rocks under her lee. But there was no staying at home. The more the wind blew, the more the pilots were needed. Not only did the cutters have to survive the weather but they also had a job of work to do. 'I have known the pilots put to sea, when to a landsman it seems sheer madness. Nothing was to be seen but a mass of broken water; nothing to be heard save the screaming of gulls, and the boom of the surf breaking on the deadly ledges.' The cutter *Agnes's* log book entry for December 1878 reads; '6 am. Strong gale with high seas; proceeded to sea.'

Apart from pilotage, salvage and rescue were part of daily life. Wrecks were frequent in the islands and an essential source of income and goods, 'looked upon as a sign of God's goodness and mercy'. Innumerable cutters went to the assistance of ships in trouble or came across a storm damaged ship drifting derelict and abandoned. One such was the *James Armstrong*, found bottom up twenty miles west of St Mary's. She was taken in tow by three cutters who brought her into the town beach. As the tide receded she was rolled over onto her side and on the next tide came upright.

There are many accounts of pilot cutters towing distressed ships into the safety of the Roads. This is dangerous work. I have towed another vessel with *Agnes* whilst under sail and, believe me, it is not a task for the faint-hearted. The tow held *Agnes* back, causing her to loose the stability gained from moving through the water. While the vessel in tow sat upright, *Agnes* had her lee rail under and I kept thinking that the next gust would lay her on her beam-ends.

Many a ship in dire straits was found whilst a cutter was on station, as the log book entries at the time illustrate:

> 2 pm 'boarded the de-masted barque *Bertha* of Liverpool in a sinking condition.'

> 3 pm 'left her expecting her to sink in a short time, all mast gone.'

> 6 am 'to the wreck of the barque *River Lune* employed about the wreck, taking on board the sails and other materials from the wreck'.

Ships coming to grief on the rocks around Scilly were a terrible constant. The tides pour through these parts with a frightening power. It seemed that every storm bought at least one victim, often many. Cutters' logbooks are full of such entries as 'Sailed through wreckage. No survivors'. This would denote yet another ship that unseen had been smashed to pieces amongst the

Wrecks were frequent in the islands and an essential source of income and goods, 'looked upon as a sign of God's goodness and mercy'.

Cutters often came across storm damaged ships drifting derelict and abandoned. If they could, the cutters would tow them in as salvage. Here such a vessel is being broken up after having been stripped of her gear on St Mary's beach.

Western Rocks. In 1862 the cutter *Presto* recovered a beautiful 6 foot long figurehead of a woman amongst wreckage being swept along on the tide.

In 1869 the St Agnes cutter *Gem*, some 80 miles west of the islands in heavy seas, spotted the three-masted *Little Lizzie*. She was clearly in trouble, with only shreds of canvas on her spars. Coming in close they launched their punt with four pilots. On gaining the ship they found her crew all lying about sick with scurvy, the first mate having only just died. The cutter set off back to Scilly for food, water, and canvas so as to help bring the *Little Lizzie* to port. The four pilots stayed aboard to manage the ship as best they could. Once the cutter was away, a gale set in from the south and blew the helpless vessel before it. On her return the *Gem* could not find the ship. The sea was empty and although they searched for several days they did not find her. Fearing the worst, they returned to Scilly, mourning the loss of their friends. However, the *Little Lizzie* drifted on, at one point close to the Irish coast, then a change of wind direction carried them towards north Cornwall. Finally, the wind calmed and they were able to get aloft and retrieve what canvas was left. With needles and twine they used this to make new sails, which they bent to the yards. Finally, weeks after they were feared lost, the four men sailed the *Little Lizzie* into port – saving the ship, its sick crew, and themselves.

There wasn't always such a happy outcome. Many a cutter or gig was lost with all hands. The island communities were close knit. Cutters were often crewed by three generations of one family. One only has to walk around the graveyard on St Agnes to see this sad toll of human life. In some cases, a father and his sons lie side by side.

Once a pilot cutter found the brig *Fortune* abandoned and sinking near the Seven Stones Reef. The cutter put aboard four of its crew in an attempt to tow the vessel into Scilly. Without warning the brig suddenly sank and it was only through swift action with an axe that the cutter was not dragged down as well. Two of the four men put aboard went down with the ship and were not seen again.

Apart from salvage, wreckage, pilotage, and free trading or bartering, the cutters also turned their hand to carrying mail and other important items to Penzance. The mail then went overland by stagecoach, reaching London long before a ship could beat up Channel. In spring the odd cargo of new potatoes would need carrying to Bristol, the cutter returning with coal from the Welsh ports.

In October the cutters were put on the beach for a refit to

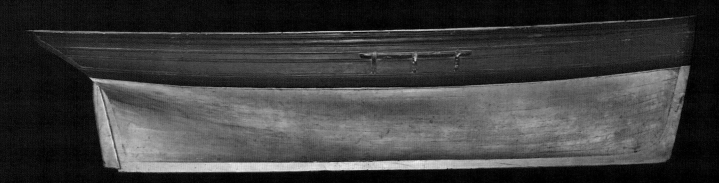

Half model of the cutter A. Z. built in 1850 by William Mumford (held in St Mary's Museum).

make them ready for the winter months. They were tarred and oiled, the rigging serviced and everything made good. The boom and topmast were unshipped and put ashore. The boomless trysail was laced to the gaff and a 'chock pole' of about 12 feet was set up through the topmast irons onto which the pilot and signal flags could be hoisted. If she survived the winter's ordeal, come the spring she would again be put ashore and the process was reversed. She would be painted up all fresh and pretty, the large summer mainsail with the 40 foot boom got back aboard, and the 40 foot topmast hoisted into place.

In August St Mary's celebrated summer with a carnival. Its main attraction was the pilot cutter and gig races. The course the cutters ran was from St Mary's Quay, north around the island, across Crow Bar, out through Crow Sound, down the

The brig James Armstrong *was found bottom up twenty miles west of St Mary's. She was taken in tow by three cutters who brought her into the town beach. As the tide receded she was rolled over onto her side and on the next tide came upright.*

Cutters often turned their hand to carrying mail and other important items to Penzance. The mail then went overland by stagecoach to London

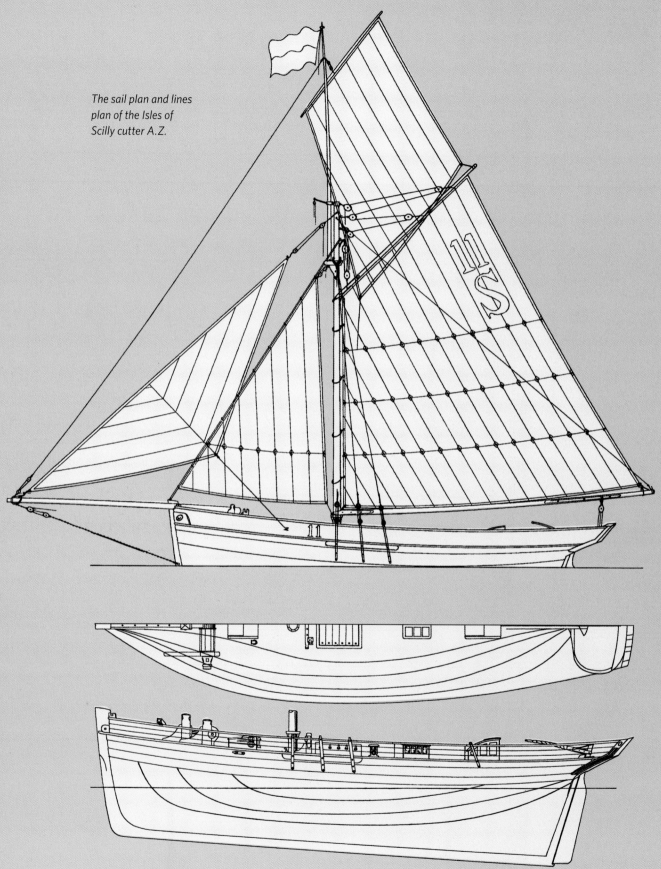

The sail plan and lines plan of the Isles of Scilly cutter A.Z.

south side of St Agnes to the Bishop Lighthouse, north of Crim Rocks, back through Broad Sound and through the Roads to St Mary's harbour – a distance of 20 nautical miles. This gave the cutters a chance to show off their sailing skills and their pilot's knowledge of the rocks and reefs that had to be negotiated in order to win. There was an immense rivalry between crews and the race was hard fought. The pride at winning the regatta would stand them in good stead for the year, as their daily lives were a race, man against man. First aboard the ship got the job.

The glory days did not last long. In the 1850s the typical cargo ship was wooden and of 400 hundred tons. Gradually their tonnage increased. Wood gave way to iron, sail to steam. By the 1870s, following the opening of the Suez Canal, for the first time more steamers were being launched from British yards than sailing ships. The smaller wooden sailing ships were driven from the deepwater trade, reducing their role to coastal trading. Within a decade the ships passing Scilly had changed beyond measure. No longer did they call in at the islands, these larger vessels preferred to await orders at Falmouth, where there was now a rail link and dry dock facilities. Tugs towed them on the short hauls between British ports, making the rounding of Lands End of little consequence. Scilly was now a place to avoid. This meant not just a loss of pilotage work but also of salvage work and the much needed revenue from bartering with ships at sea or victualling of them in St Mary's Roads. A vain attempt to revive the islands' fortunes was made by setting up a coaling-station for bunkering the steamers, and, in 1872, the telegraph was brought to the isles. But by this time there was no stopping the change. By the 1880s 3,000 ton steamers dominated the Western Approaches. It was all over. 'Nothing to be seen of any homeward bound ships,' wrote one pilot cutter captain in his logbook.

Competition became cut-throat. Falmouth cutters worked far beyond Scilly. The port's 15 cutters were larger and faster vessels, and would shadow the smaller Scillonian cutters, deploying a tactic of boxing in the Scilly cutters on all four points of the compass, so as not to allow access to incoming ships.

Although it was too late to save the Scillonian pilots, the situation was alleviated somewhat in 1887. Aware that too many cutters were chasing too few ships, Trinity House decided to rationalise the pilotage service around the coast. The Falmouth and St Mawes boats were amalgamated and bought under joint ownership and the number of boats was cut to eleven. Thereafter, all the member pilots shared equally in the group earnings, cutting out the fights between rival men over

Captain Steven Jenkins ,'Ste' of the cutter Agnes, *grandfather of our good friend Alf who launched the new* Agnes.

who took the ship. Simultanously, their cruising ground was reduced to a sea area from the Lizard Point to Dodman Point. With this change their methods of hailing a ship changed also. From now on the ship came to the boat, with the cutter staying on station, normally off the Lizard.

Because of the new practise of sharing proceeds equally, there was no longer a need for the cutters to race in order to make certain that their pilot boarded first. The large rig with its unwieldy boom, mainsail, and topsail was redundant. Pilots now set their winter trysail and small jibs all year round, making the cutters easier to handle. For this reason most surviving photographs of Falmouth cutters show them setting the loose-footed trysail and 'choke pole'.

Like the Scillies, Falmouth cutters developed many ways of supplying incoming shipping. Tailors and grocers bought

Left: *The Falmouth cutter* Arrow *on Grove Place Beach, and below the* Vincent *on Bar Beach.*

Above & below: *In 1887 the Falmouth cutters were amalgamated. After this the cutters only set their winter rig, getting rid of their big unwieldy booms – hence why the* Vincent *is here sailing with her boomless trysail.*

cutters. In 1857 R. T. McMullen fell into conversation with a tailor's cutter when both were becalmed off the Lizard. The tailors proudly told him that it was his practise to board 'homeward bound ships to supply clothes to those who preferred walking ashore in a new suit, to being seen in sea-stained garments.' McMullen wished them well, noting that 'a more civil set of men he never chanced to meet.' Sadly, eleven years later this same tailor's cutter was running for Falmouth during a gale when heavy seas broke on board off the Manacles, sweeping the captain to his death.

At the beginning of the 1880s there were still nine Scillonian cutters at work. By 1887 there were four, by 1890 only one, the *Agnes*. The cutters *Presto* and *Atlantic* of St Mary's were sold off to pilots in Milford Haven. The *Queen* and *Argus* were put ashore on St Martin's to rot and the *Rapid* and *A.Z.* of Bryher were broken up to be used as fencing and windbreaks in the fields.

Flower growing now gave the pilots their livelihood. In early spring the daffodils were sent 'ashore' to the mainland. There are poignant old photographs of once proud pilots still in their sea going gear, bent over in the flower fields picking daffodils.

Only the *Agnes* carried on as best she could. By the end of the century she earned her keep carrying new potatoes to the mainland, returning with coal for the greenhouses.

Finally, in 1902, too tired to carry on trading, she was broken up on Tresco and used for fencing. Even with *Agnes* gone the men always kept half an eye on the sea and at the sight of a sail on the horizon would put off in their gigs to see if they could be of service. But they did so more out of habit and for old times sake, for the days of the pilots were over.

Above: *Vincent cruising out in the bay, with the Channel fleet at anchor.*
Below: *This is a most important photo taken in 1876, nine years before the amalgamation, and shows the Falmouth pilot cutters No 3 the* Vie *and No 11 the* Nautilus *with their booms and large mainsail.*

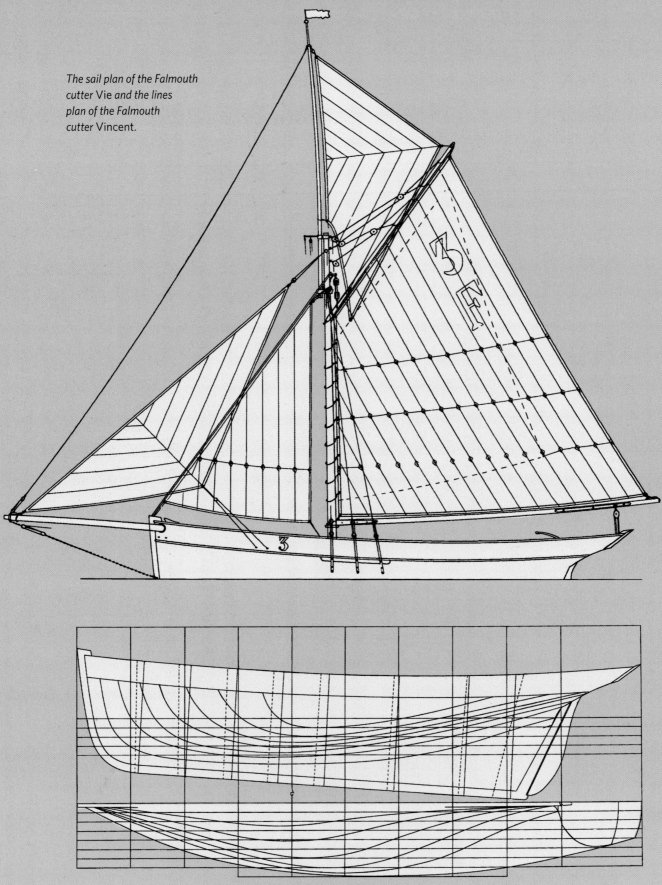

The sail plan of the Falmouth cutter Vie *and the lines plan of the Falmouth cutter* Vincent.

They turned 'Easting home', along Latitude 49½ N, heading for the Western Approaches. The night was long the weather was stormy, as the southwesterly wind briskly pushed them onwards. Never knowing from where would land would appear?

Glossary

Arch-board The timber that traverses the counter from side to side at deck level.

Bawley A type of sailing fishing boat in the Thames estuary that had a boomless cutter rig,transom stern, and had a boiler for cooking shrimp amidships.

Beam shelf A thick plank around the inside of a boat that supports the deck beams.

Bilge Inside the bottom of a boat, where any water that accumulates can then be pumped out.

Bits The upright posts in the bow of a boat that hold the inboard end of the bowsprit.

Bow thruster A propeller set in the bow so that it can push the boat from side to side, for people that do not have any knowledge of seamanship.

Bulwarks The wooden walls around a boat above deck.

Cut down When a sailing vessel has a motor fitted and the rig reduced to an auxiliary role.

Caught in Irons When a boat is in the process of tacking and gets stuck head to wind and so can't manouevre.

Cable A hundred fathoms or 600 feet or one tenth of a nautical mile.

Carlins The fore and aft part of the deck-beam structure that edges an opening for a hatch.

Channels Horizontal chocks of wood, on the outside of a vessel just below deck level that spread the shrouds.

Coamings The structural sides of a hatch, they sit on top of the carling and are through bolted.

Chain plates The iron straps that go down vertically each side of the hull upon which the shrouds are attached.

Clench A rod that is driven through an assemblage of wood and riveted over a washer on each side.

Centre line The wooden structure that is composed of the keel, stem, and stern posts including deadwoods: in all the backbone of the boat.

Covering board The margin-board around the deck that gives strength to the corner of hull and deck, and through which the stanchions are fitted.

Deadwood The large knee assemblies that strengthen the connection of the stem and stern-post to the keel.

Doubling Either a thicker plank around a boat that gives strength and acts as a fender or where an extra layer of planking is put on the hull to take the chafing of either fishing gear or where the hull takes the ground.

Dumps Lengths of rod with a head forged at one end used to pin large timbers together, like a giant nail. Blind dumps are the same but without a head and set into the hole.

Double sawn frames Frames that are made up of two layers connected together with staggered butts.

The Downs An anchorage inside the Goodwin Sands off the Kentish coast used by ships waiting a fair wind.

Edge set When a plank is cut out straighter that it should be, and then has to be pulled up or down to fit the gap.

Ekki A tropical hardwood that is found up the Congo (*Lophira alata*).

Fathom Six feet.

Fantail counter A type of counter that is wide and flat with a sloping transom and looks rather like the tail or a dove.

Fiddled top mast A top mast that is raised through two iron hoops at the top of the main mast and is a separate spar that can be lowered.

Forefoot The part of the bow where the stem meets the keel.

Futtock A curve shaped timber in the framing of the hull.

Garboard strake The plank adjacent to the keel.

Gammon-iron A round hoop attached to the stem through which the bowsprit fits.

Hogged Where an old vessel starts to sag at the ends and loose its shape. The middle of the boat is buoyant and the ends are not, so the middle rises up while the ends drop down.

Horn-timbers The timbers on the counter that project aft to give the counter its length.

Glossary

Hood ends The plank ends that fit against the stem or stern posts.

Hounds At the top part of the mast, the cheeks and trestle trees that serve to support the shrouds.

Knights heads The timber that rises up each side of the stem, giving strength to the bow where the sprit and hawse pipes are fitted.

Lofting Where one draws out the plan of the boat in full size on a floor, so that the frames can be made directly on the drawing.

Land The face of the frame where the plank will sit.

League Three nautical miles. Originally it referred to the distance a person or a horse could walk in an hour.

Lengthening a boat Where a vessel is cut in half and pulled apart. A new section is then built into the middle to increase the boat's length

Lodging knees A wooden knee that is built into the boat horizontally between the deck beams to strengthen the connection between deck and hull.

Lute stern A type of stern that has a transom that leans back in a curve with the rudder coming up through it. This design went out of fashion by the 1860s.

Maul A shipwright's hammer with a long handle. The back of the head is pointed so that when used this way round it can set nails home.

Oak bends Slabs of an oak tree that have a natural bend, which can be used to cut out the frames of a vessel.

Opepe A hard wood from West Africa (*Nauclea diderrichii*) used in structural work such as bridges or boats.

Paying When you pour hot pitch into the seams on the deck of a boat.

Punt A largish dinghy used as a tender to sailing vessels such as cutters and schooners.

Planer-thicknesser A woodworking machine that can plane off a surface, so that a plank can be reduced to a said thickness.

Quarter-timber The knees that project aft on each sides of the counter.

Rudder trunk The wooden barrel-like tube that allows the rudder up through the counter.

Setting home When the nails in the planks of a boat are driven below the surface, so that they can be hidden with plugs or stopping.

Scantlings The scale and dimensions of a boat's timbers.

Shutter plank The last plank to be fitted to a new boat.

Sheer The curve of a vessel's deck line.

Sheer strake The top plank on a boat that defines the sheer of the boat.

Strake A plank in the hull of a boat.

Spiel To take the measurements from the hull with the use of a batten that is laid into a space, these measurements are then transferred to the board from which a plank can be cut to fit this space.

Spike A boat nail, normally square in section and galvanized.

Spritsail A type of mainsail that is held out with a diagonal spar that goes from the mast at deck level to the top outer corner.

Stanchions Upright posts around the edge of the deck that carries the bulwarks and rail.

Sticking the wood When one puts small battens between planks in a stack, creating gaps that allow air to circulate

Stopping The putty that is pushed into seams on the hull of a boat.

Tar Planer A hand-held electric plane, the name comes from the first company to make them.

Thicknessed When a plank is planed down to a said thickness.

Turfer A ratchet winch that pulls on a wire.

Tuck The curve of the hull under the stern.

Running lights The red and green navigation lights

Topgallant rails The extra rail that sits on top of the bulwarks above the capping rail.

Top strake The top most plank on the hull defining the deck level.

Acknowledgements

There are a lot of people I would like to thank, but my largest debt is to wife Joanna for all the help she gave me in working on the text and turning it into readable English – as well as for putting up with the endless evenings in which I relived my past. Christian Topf had the vision to believe that together we could make a good book. David Burnett was brave enough to take a gamble with me, and also had the stoicism to work through my ramblings.

I owe an enormous debt to those who have had sufficient faith in me to buy a Working Sail boat, and to all those who helped build them – there are too many to list them all, but the core team were Jonny Albrecht, James Baker and Andy Cornish.

I would like to thank Tom Cunliffe and Jeremy Irons for their friendship and support in writing forewords for the book, Gillian and Clive Emerson for helping me set up at Gweek, Alf Jenkins for supporting my research into Scillonan pilot cutters and helping launch the boats, and Jonny Albrecht, John Gryphon and David Willcox for the hours spent proofreading the text.

Most of the illustrations come from my own collection, but I must thank all those who, over the years, have given me photographs which now appear in this book. Unfortunately it is difficult to remember the origins of each photograph, but I thank all of them from the bottom of my heart. The following I know of, and I would like to thank them for their kindness in providing illustrations: Nick Beck, Jenny Bennett, Ralph Bird, Sam and Ingrid Brooks, Martin Burton, Andrew Campbell, Anna Cattermole, Ann Marie Colbert, The Cornish Studies Library - Redruth, R.A. Dorien Smith, Richard East, Sandra Gibson (Gibsons of Scilly), David Glenn and IPC Media, Basil Greenhill, Ken Hayse, Jerry Headle, Alf Jenkins, Gillard Johnson, Ester Lewis, Steve Miller, Adam and Debbie Purser, Alan and Rhondda Reekie, Lena Reekie, Royal Cornwall Polytechnic Society, Falmouth, Mike Smylie, Mark Stainer, Sara Stirling, Christian Topf and Alf Trenear.

Appendix 2 was compiled with the help of previous research done by Ralph Bird, Alf Jenkins, R. T. McMullen, and Sara Stirling, to whom I am truly grateful.

Amanda Martin at the Isle of Scilly Museum, St Mary's, kindly allowed me to take the lines off the half model of a Scillonian pilot cutter, and Ralph Bird generously did the same with his half model of a Falmouth pilot cutter.

List of Subscribers

The publisher would like to thank all those whose names are listed below, as well as the subscribers who chose to remain anonymous. Their support helped make this book possible.

The Airlies
Ralph Allardyce
Penny Allen
Barry Almond
Mike Andrews, Haines Boatyard, Itchenor
Michael Guy Ankers
Annabel J
Konstantin Anori
Colin Appleby
Lez and Christine Arkell
M.W. Ashworth

M.J.C. Bailey
Roger Bailey
John Baker
Nick Baker
Nigel Baker
David Balfour
Bryan Barnes
Roger W. Baxter
Nick Beck and Melisa Collett
Michael Bender
Peter J. Bensley
Sarah Bibra
Robin Bishop
R.J. Blemming
Anouk Bloch
Mark Bonsall
Ken Boullier
Philip A. Boulton
David Bowers
Susan Bowker
Andy Bozson
Ann Marie and Victor Bradley (*Tallulah*)
Arthur Paul Bredin
Paul Brightmore
Sam, Ingrid and Morag Brooke
Edward Brooks
Simon and Lucy Brooks
J.H.M. Brown
Iain and Wilma Bruce
George Buchanan
Richard Varian Buckland
Terry Bullard
James Bullock
Simon Bunker

Robert Burge
Ron Burgin
Jeremy Burnett
Ken Burnige
Butler & Co

Richard Callingham
Andrew Camp
Colin and Heather Campbell
John Cann
Mark and Loz Cann
Sarah and Brian Carbry
Shane Carr
Phil Carter
Anna Cattermole
Ralph Cawthorne
Craig Chad
D.P. Chadwick
Michael Chapman
Thomas R. Christopherson
Peter Clare
M. Clark
Steve Clarke from Gweek
Tim Clayson
Richard Clowes
Michael von Collas
Jim Collett
William Collinson
Paul Connor
D. Cornelius
Ralph Courtie
Gerry and Sue Cox
Steve 'Skipper' Craston
Richard Creighton
Philip Crockatt
Graham Cross
John Crossman
Ian Curphey
Iain John Curphey
Peter Cuthbertson

John Daley
Tim Daniel
Hugh Darlington
The Davidson Family
Michael Davies
John F. Dawson
Jonathan Frank Day

Dennis Debbage, Suffolk Boatbuilder
Chris Deighton
Damien Leroux de Lens
John Norton Denner
James Dodds
Jan Doets
Glennis Lauren Dore
Nick Downing
Ian Drewry
Daniel Duff
Alan J. Dunn – V.W.B.A.

Ralph K. Eade
The Reverend Andrew J. Earl CF
Richard East
Neil Eatough
John Eddy
Sally-Ann Edlin
Michael Ramsay Edmonds
Mrs. Pamela J. Edsall
Frank J. Edwards
Toby Elliott
Chris Elzakkers
Paul Endicott
Tish Ennis

Ian and Jeanie Falconer
Ian J. Farr
Beryl and Sid Fisher
Graeme Fisher
Simon Fletcher
G.K. Forrest
Robin Forrest
Stephen Forster
I.D. Foster
Tim and Alison Fraser
Bernard Funston

Anthony Gale
Colin Galloway
Michael Gaskell
Neil George
Mick Gibbs
Nick Gilbert
Claire Giles
Alexander Goldsmith
Judi Goodchild

Andrew E. Goodwin
Mickey Googh
Robert James Gorman
Jeffrey Gouk
Nick Graham
Brian and Nick Graves
Julian Gray-Read
David Nevin Greatrex
Richard Grieve
Ralph Griffith
Marcus Griffiths
Marcello Grillini

C.J. Hagstrom
Stephen J. Hall
Ian S. Hamilton
Thomas C. Hamlin, Metaphor Craft
Steve Hammond
Janie Harford and James Dodd
Philip A.T. Hargreaves
Neil Harper
Ski and Anthony Harrison
Tracey Hart
Kim Hartley – *Polly Agatha*
Nick Harvey
Peter F. Harvey
Chris Harwood
Bea Hawkins
Jim Hazel (Retired Principal Lecturer Yacht Manufacturing Technology and Boatyard Management)
Thomas Head
Jerry Headley
Chris Heape
Ronald Henderson
Frank A.A. Hennessy
M. Herbert
Ray Hewitt
Tim Hextall
Alfred Hicks
Andrew Hill
Mark Hillman
Alan T. Hinds
Åge Hjortland
Kevin John Hodges
Simon Hodgson
Trygve Hoff

Rod Holliman
Derek Holman
Roger Holzmacher
Liam Hopkins
Deirdre Hoyle
Thomas Huber
Mervyn Huggett
Ben Hulmston
Ed Hume
Andrew Hunt
Pam and Alan Hunt
Alan Hutchinson

Chris Jackson
Joep Jacobs
John and Sally Jacques
Christopher James
Ellen-Louisa James
Lilli James
Mark Jardine
Ben Jefferies
Dr. Richard Jeffery
Anders and Marion Johnson,
	s/v *Freya*
Charles Joly
Chris Jones
Gareth Jones

Mrs. Elwyn Kaye
Bruce Keefauver
Edward Kemp
Colin Kendall-Torry
Damon Kenneil
David Kent
Paul Devereux King
Richard Kirkby
Clive Knight
Themistoklis Kouvarakis
Jaap Kraayenhof
Anders Kristensen, Denmark
Matthias Krueger

Robert Lankester
Trevor Lansley, Sheerline Marine
Ken and Sonya Leaman
Nick Le Dieu
Boyd Lee
Michael A.J. Lee
Lars Lehmann
Richard and Debbie Lemon
Letty, 1905 Pilot Cutter
Nina Lillie
Stuart Little
Jonathan Lloyd
David Longville
Uilliam O. Lorcáin
Vic Love
Ian M. Lowe

Fredrik Lundahl

Robert MacAndrew
James Macfarlane
James R. MacGregor
J.D. Marine
Simon Marshall
Stanton D. Marsland
Mascotte
Christopher Mayhead
Mr. Shaun Mayland
David McGuinness
Rachel McMullen and David
	Titterington
Ken Metcalf
David Metherell
Andrew Mitchell
Anthony C. Mitchell
Fiona Molloy
John Moorshead
Stephen Morris
David Mortlock
David Moss
Mike Mowlam
John Mullins
Chris and Sharon Murphy
Rob Murray
Paul Myatt

John Nadin
Gregory Nasmyth
Polly Ness
Tristan Ness
Stephen 'Hooks' Noonan

Robert Olive
Phil Oliver
Philip and Jan Oliver

Daren Scott Packham
Neil Parkinson
John D Parnell
David Parr
Stephen Parry
David Paynter
A.C.S. Payton
Jessica Pearson
Tony Pease
Gilbert Pépin
Allison and Ron Pfister-Dwileski
Martin Phillips
Jeffrey V.W. Please
James Poole
Neal Poston
Robin Pote
Alexander Potts
John M. Powell
Robert Powell

Susanna Powell
Mark Prewett
Dave Priddle
Emanuele Puccinelli
Debbie Purser

A.J. Raffray
Michael Randall
Iain Rawlinson
Fiona Read
Anthony Readhead
Carol Readhead
Red Gauntlet
Alan Reekie
Lena Reekie
Brian Reeves (restoring *Amaryllis*)
Raymond Reynolds
Terry Reynolds
David Richards
Charles Richardson
Dave Rickett
Robert Ritchie
Christine Roberts
Vic Robinson
Jason Robinson-Gay
Rochester Independent College
J.C. Roddick
Diccon Stideford Rogers
Mark Rothwell
Bernie Rowe

Rodney Charles Salzman
Peter Samuel
Chris Savage
Brian T. Scott
Bernard Sealy
Howard Sharp
Dr. G.J. Sherwood
Trevor Silver
Peter Sigston Simmons
Robert Maxwell Sinclair
Colin Antony Slade
A.J.A. Sluce
David Smith (*Rogue 21*)
Nick Smith
Mike Smylie
Stephen Snaith
Richard Sowman
Colin Speedie and Louise Johnson
Jonathan Spencer
Jay Stainer
Mark Stainer
Richard Stephenson
Chris Stevens – Yacht *Finlandia*
Paul Stickley
Richard Stone
Paul Stopps
Anthony Sutcliffe

Mark A. Sutherland
Stephen Swabey
Anders Swahn, in memory of
	Hans Swahn
Katherine Syred

Sandy Taggart
Jonathan Tatlow
Ben and Holly Taylor
Richard Taylor
Fitsum Tefera
Catherine and Chris Thomas
Jim Thomson
Malcolm Thomson
Jørgen Tilma
Geoffrey Todd
Phil Townsend
Huw Traylor
Geoff Trebilcock
Roland Trott
Vivienne Turner
David Twyman

Cyril Varley
Roger Vaughan
John Vickers

Michael Wakefield
John Wallace
David Walsh
Shel Wappler
Revd. Canon Lionel Webber
D.W.D. Weir
Adrian Wheatley
Andrew Wheatley
James Wheeler
David Whiley
Chris Wickham
Andrew Wilkes
Jim Wilkinson
David and Kathryn Willcox
Andrew Douglas Williams
John Williams
T.J. Williams
Tony Williams
Peter Willis
Alastair J. Wilson (*Paola*)
Guy Wilson
Ian D. Wilson
Nicholas Winkfield
Mr. Ross Winmill
Tony Winter
Jane Wright
Mark Wright
Dick Wynne
Jon Yorke
Lt. Commander T.F.B. Young,
	RN Retired